TAKE WHAT YOU NEED

TAKE WHAT YOU NEED

Life Lessons after Losing Everything

JEN CROW

BROADLEAF BOOKS
MINNEAPOLIS

TAKE WHAT YOU NEED
Life Lessons after Losing Everything

This book is a work of nonfiction based in my memory. Memory is imperfect, and the stories told here are based on my perspective and colored by the events of my life. Events and dialogue are constructed from memory and should not be taken as verbatim accounts. While all of the stories are true, based on real people I've known and loved, I imagine some of the people in these stories have a different perspective from what I share here. When other peoples' memories differ from what I've recounted here, I welcome those viewpoints, trusting that additional perspectives only enrich the story, adding layers of new meaning for us all.

Lastly, each of the people portrayed in this book are human, and being human is tricky business. I believe that everyone in these stories was doing the best that they could in incredibly difficult circumstances. I hope that no matter what other thoughts or feelings may come up as you read, you will also experience the humanity of each individual, and my love and care for them all.

Cover design: Laywan Kwan

Print ISBN: 978-1-5064-6861-7
eBook ISBN: 978-1-5064-6862-4

With gratitude for everyone who nurtured and protected the light inside of me over the years, and especially for my family, Loretta, Henry, and Kate, who proved to me once and for all that we can get through anything if we do it together.

CONTENTS

Part III
Hold it all

INTRODUCTION

This book began with a fire, but it didn't take long for other life experiences of loss and disruption to come crowding in. The fires in my life have been both literal and metaphorical, and all of them left me asking and answering similar questions in moments of challenge and loss.

All of us know something about fires—those events that change everything in an instant. For me, whenever one hits, I find myself seeking a small, private place to meet the sudden news with my own version of grief. Usually, it's a bathroom floor.

After our house fire, it wasn't my own bathroom floor, because in those early days nothing was our own. We were borrowing pants and places to sleep, accepting meals and money, wearing clothes that kind of fit and saying thank you for it all.

Sleeping didn't come easily to me in those first days, so after everyone was tucked into bed and snoring softly, I'd sneak into the bathroom and settle myself down on the floor, back to the wall, head in my hands, crying as quietly as I could. With all of my beloveds on the other side of that sliding pocket door, I let out what I couldn't show them, tears running hot down my face. I couldn't let them know how hard this hit. Couldn't let them know that I was falling apart. They had already left our home in the middle of the night with only the clothes on their backs; they didn't need to see me cry. They needed to hear me say that everything was going to be alright. That I'd get us back home. That we were okay.

And during the day, I did just that. I fought with the insurance company. I packed up boxes. I found our important papers and dried them in the sun. I showed up after school to greet the kids with smiles and a snack. I dug through the debris for their blankets. I bought them new shoes. And, of course, I didn't do any of this alone. My wife did it, too. Our friends showed up in droves. Our church lifted us up.

And still, alone and awake in the middle of the night, I'd sneak out of bed, sick of restless rest, and make my way to the bathroom floor. In those moments, I couldn't bear to reach out. Couldn't stand the idea of waking someone up or sending a text even though I knew there were good people all around me who wished I would. Anyone who has experienced the tunnel of trauma knows that things can narrow down and make it hard to see the fullness of the world all around you. That was happening to me. I longed for connection—but I couldn't access it.

I turned to god. After all, as a minister, that's the expected starting point, right? But praying was hard. Gratitude and rage, despair, fear, and disappointment swirled in me. I was glad that we were alive. I knew it could have been otherwise. And yet the stability I'd spent my life striving to build felt suddenly lost. I had a hard time getting to god.

I turned to poetry—to the words that had carried me through so many hard nights before. Nancy Shaffer's "A Theology Adequate for the Night" kept me company each night on that bathroom floor.

A Theology Adequate for the Night

By Nancy Shaffer

Not God as unmoved mover:
One who set the earth in motion
and withdrew. Not
the one to thank
when those cherished
do not die—
for providence includes equally
power to harm. Not a
God of exactings,
as if love could be
earned or subtracted.

But—this may work in
the night:
something that
breathes with us, as
others
sleep, something that
breathes also those sleeping, so no
one is alone.
Something that is
the beginning of love,
and also each part of how love is completed.

Something so large,
wherever we are,
we are not separate;
which teaches again
the way to start over.

Night is the test:
when grief lies uncovered,
and longing shows
clear; when nothing
we do
can hasten earth's
turning or delay it.

This may be adequate
for the night:
this holding: something
that steadfastly
breathes us, which we
also are learning to breathe.

When my breath went ragged, hitching and heaving with the fear, I'd imagine some thing, some love, that could breathe with me as others slept, that breathed also with those sleeping, so that none of us were alone. I'd breathe in and out, trying to trust that the world was breathing with me.

And when that wasn't enough or I got bored—because come on, this is the twenty-first century and I still had my phone—I did what we all do: scour the internet for books or blogs or anything that might relate to our circumstances. There were a few small things here or there, but nothing substantive. Nothing that went beyond tips for working with your insurance company or getting through the first two days of shock. I desperately wanted a survival story to keep me company in the night, some reassurance that one day I, too, might have my own.

So, dear reader, this is that story for me—and for you. My experience will be different from your own, and what helps you may be different from what helped me. Not everyone will come to this book having experienced a house fire, but most of you will know what it's like to experience loss. To have the world as you knew it, with all of your hopes and expectations, crumble when the diagnosis or the death comes, when the lover leaves, when the change—be it welcome or unwanted—arrives. Our journeys are unique. Our resources may not be the same, and the weight of systemic oppression may land differently on your shoulders. But whoever we are, it can help to have company as we travel.

Born on the bathroom floor in the middle of the night, this book is one version of my story of survival. I hope it will keep you company as you write your own.

Part 1

Notice, you

For you who thought it would never be rebuilt, the pieces never found, the structure never sound

For you who worried your family and spirit had been torn apart, never to knit back together again

For you who lost so much—the expectation of safety in the night, first day of kindergarten, old photographs all gone

For you who wondered if you'd ever feel whole again

For you who wondered and worried how this story would turn out

Notice, you.

Notice the firm couch beneath you that sits on the beautiful wood floor, gleaming and scratched by the dog's too-long toenails

Notice your grandmother's buffet, refinished and strong, an anchor of weight and history flanking you, family silver tucked inside, polished to gleaming by the hands of friends and strangers

TAKE WHAT YOU NEED

Notice the pictures of your children smiling on top of it

Notice your favorite leather chair sitting under the window that frames the lilac tree you planted, a gift as you moved home, marking your own new beginning

Notice the relief you feel, the result of hours of effort and the cleansing power of tears

Notice how your children sleep soundly in their own beds most of the nights now, and so do you

Notice this
here
now
A web of kindness and care is visible that had gone unseen before

Notice and breathe this clean air
No smoke, no mold, no water here
Clean, clear, air

Notice your home,
you're home.

Chapter 1

Take What You Need...

What would you grab on the way out the door if your house was on fire?

Publications like *Forbes* and agencies like the Federal Emergency Management Agency (FEMA) make super practical lists you can consult, but they don't seem to have any grasp on reality, as far as I can see. They tell you to grab your documents and essential items—licenses, passports, checkbooks, hard drives, insurance policies, birth certificates, IDs, and medication. They tell you that if you really have your act together, you'll keep all of these documents plus a full inventory of every item in your house in a tiny fireproof safe that you can just pick up and calmly carry out of your burning house. Really, they actually say this. Go buy your tiny fireproof safe today.

The truth is, these lists are ridiculous. They don't tell you anything you need to know. But I will. When your house catches on fire, like mine did, if you have any time to do anything but survive . . .

Put on a decent pair of shoes. Flip-flops might seem like a great idea at the time, but they suck the next day when you are walking through the wet and poky rubble of your life.

Grab your phone. Nobody memorizes phone numbers anymore, and god knows you are going to need your friends.

Grab your car keys, the dog leash, your glasses, and the dog.

But first, pull your partner and your children out of their beds. Don't ever leave them behind, even if you have to carry them out in flip-flops.

Standing out in the rain, listen to your partner when she tells you that whatever comes in the days ahead, don't ever forget that we all walked out of that house.

When the fire is out and the firefighters come to let you back into the house, go for your wedding rings, the necklace your grandmother always wore that you wear now when you need to feel her love close around you. Go for the stuffed animals your children used to sleep with, safe in their beds. And definitely find a bra. You'll be meeting with a lot of people these next few days.

Grab your son's homework—the papers he so diligently filled out sitting at the dining room table just hours before. Watch the water and the soot roll off the pages as you lift them from under the tarp the firefighters so thoughtfully draped over the table where you ate breakfast and dinner. Remember the day you moved into the house and worried that the hot pizza boxes you'd just put on the new table would leave a mark on the fresh finish. Wish for the problems of that day.

Pull the photographs out of the cabinet—notice for a fleeting moment the irony of wrapping your most precious memories in white plastic garbage bags with red pull ties and quietly carry them to your car, where your dog has been waiting, wondering what the hell is going on as he paces back and forth, quiet, for once, as his whole world turns upside down, too.

Notice your neighbor, your daughter in his arms and your son holding tight to his hand as they walk away from the house and into his family's embrace of safety and strength. Say yes when they offer to pack your kids' lunches for school the next day.

When your friends pull up in front of your still-smoldering house, let them take the phone when the insurance agent asks again about the extent of the damage. Let them drive when it's time to leave. Let them tuck your kids into their beds, their own children scooting over and holding little hands until all of them fall asleep. Let them braid your daughter's hair the next morning, stopping you to insist on first-day-of-kindergarten photos by the tree in their front yard.

Each night after the fire, scoop up your family and hold them close to your chest. Your heart is going to pound harder than you can imagine in the days and nights ahead, and you are going to need each other. You are going to need to remember that it could be so much worse as you bury your head in your partner's chest, as your children collapse into you, their breathing finally changing from heaving sobs to slow inhaling and exhaling to deep, improbable sleep. You will keep moving because you have them—going out to meet the contractors, finding a new place to live, collecting receipts in a giant envelope. You will show up, keeping things moving when all you want to do is lie down and cry because your family needs you to make things right again.

You will smile at the well-meaning people who want to draw a smiley face on your sadness, brushing away the ones who tell you that if you had just had a lightning rod or a shorter house or a taller house or a different house this wouldn't have happened to you. Don't fall for their lies, their need to control, manage, and contain this loss. You know the truth now, that life is not that neat, that loss comes to all of us whether we are prepared or not. Drop the illusion of the tiny fireproof safe, filled with the lie that this loss could somehow, someway have been contained or controlled. The loss is big. The pain is real. The safe would not have helped.

It helped me to remember that we all walked out of that house, that we each managed to recover a couple of the items that meant the most to us. And what I could not have known then was that what we needed was never inside that house. What we needed was outside the house: in people we knew and didn't know yet, in the web I never saw so clearly before—the web of people present, past, and future who would hold my family in love and would not let us go. The web that would tremble and break in places but ultimately hold strong and reknit, reweave the broken places into a new reality. Even when we thought all was lost, even when the pain brought us to our knees, what we needed was never inside that house.

So when the lightning strikes, take what *you* need. Trust that what helps you survive the inevitable losses in life will be different from what helped me survive or what FEMA promises is most important. What helped me is not what helped my wife, and what my kids needed is only some of what I needed. People will have all kinds of advice and ideas for you, many of them unhelpful and unwanted, many of them directed at what might make this particular loss easier for them.

What we probably all need is someone who can actually listen to what our unique experience is like. People who can sit next to us when there are no words, who can suggest things and then let them go if they aren't quite right or follow through when they hit the mark. People who can hear the pain without rushing in to fix it. What we need is safety and shelter and whatever comfort looks like to us.

My hope for all of us is that we will have what we need. To discover a web of love so big it can hold us and the reality of our unique losses. To let go of the lists and the advice that so many others have for us, and take what we need.

Chapter 2

. . . And Leave the Rest Behind

If you've decided to pick up this book, chances are you know what it is to have your life change in an instant. One day things were one way, and the next day they were different. Maybe it wasn't a literal bolt of lightning, but something shifted. It happens to all of us. The love, the loss, the change, the risk, success, and failure. The wailing, the cheering, the relief, and the grief. Our lives are full of events that have the power to change us, and as we tell our stories, we claim the power to determine just how we will be changed.

In the days after our house fire, I realized that our kids were taking their cues from us. They were listening in on the conversations the adults were trying to have in the other room, and I wanted them to hear our gratitude, not our fear. I wanted them to remember the helpers, the deck of cards and the pan of chocolate-chip cookies that arrived that first week with a note from the only other family we knew who'd survived a house fire, letting us know that even though we couldn't imagine it yet, our world would feel safe again someday. I wanted them to notice how we always had what we needed even when we lost everything. I wanted them to be able to acknowledge the pain and the loss, to feel the grief, and to come out on the other side with gratitude.

And I knew that if we were going to get from grief to gratitude, we were going to have to do it on purpose. The pain was simply too much to expect that time alone could heal us. My wife and I needed to be intentional about how we told the story of our fire because we knew our kids were listening. And, as usual, those things that the kids needed? Turns out we needed them, too.

My seminary training taught me that any event could carry meaning, and we'd need to be careful what meaning this event would come to hold. Old ideas surprised me, and I found we needed to say out loud that the lightning was not some sort of punishment. This random event wasn't some sort of cosmological joke or irrefutable proof that hardship never ends. And it certainly wasn't a god-driven conspiracy to keep me from ever going back to the gym or getting a moment to myself. It was a bolt of lightning—morally neutral electricity that could have struck anywhere but happened to strike our house. There was nothing we could have done to predict or control it coming. But how it would change us and the meaning we would make? That would be up to us.

"We think we tell stories, but stories often tell us," writes Rebecca Solnit in *The Faraway Nearby*.

> Often, too often, stories saddle us, whip us onward, tell us what to do, and we do it without questioning. The task of learning to be free requires learning to hear them, to question them, to pause and hear silence, to name them, and then to become the storyteller.

Telling and retelling the story of our fire, I've learned that the language I use matters. The facts I choose to collect and magnify change the meaning. What started with a push away from the stories other people were telling about our house fire turned into bigger questions about other experiences in my life and the world. And I began to wonder if more than one version of a story can be true at the same time. If we can hold grief and gratitude all in the same breath.

Some of the best advice I ever received was this: "In whatever situation you find yourself, take what you need and leave the rest behind." Don't waste your energy arguing. Just take what you need and leave the rest behind. Over the years, I've found this advice works not only for family gatherings and twelve-step meetings but for the larger project of spiritual living, too. And the best news of all: this taking what we need and leaving the rest behind isn't only a one-time thing. We can do it anytime. Looking back over our lives, we can hear the stories anew, choosing where to focus our attention and where to widen our view. We can let go of old ways of understanding that no longer serve us and we can wiggle our way free, becoming the meaning makers and the storytellers of our own lives. We get to choose what we need in a given moment. And what we need gets to change.

When my first marriage ended in divorce, I told myself that all I needed was my new last name and a spatula. But that was a short take on a longer story. The truth was, I needed a whole lot more.

When it all ended, I was stunned. I never wanted to be someone who was married and then divorced. I wanted to be dependable. Predictable. Loyal. I wanted to be someone who hung in there no matter what. I wanted to be the person dedicated to building a life together, not dissolving promises. But there we were, acknowledging the undeniable fact that we had grown in different directions. That we loved each other but were no longer good for each other.

At twenty-nine years old, I found myself standing in front of the apartment we once shared with a death grip on a rubber spatula. I'm pretty sure I looked like I had lost my mind. And I had. My friends swarmed around me like bees. They set to the work of finding this and that, of taping up boxes and tucking them into pockets of space in the truck so we could get in and out before my newly ex-wife came home. And before I killed this guy in the driveway.

"You know you can't park here, right?" he said as he made his way toward me. Maybe he was too far away to notice my red-rimmed eyes or the tears I'd been trying to keep clear from my cheeks. Or maybe he was just an asshole.

"Moving has to be done through the back doorway, not the front.

You didn't tell the association you were doing this, did you?

Didn't you read the lease?

You have to tell the association whenever someone moves in or out so they can hang those blankets up in the elevator so you don't scuff the walls.

There's going to be a fee for this."

As he marched in my direction, he fired word after word. I took a deep breath, willing myself not to react in a way I would regret later.

As my marriage was ending, I had one mantra: don't do anything you are going to have to apologize for later. I could pretend that this mantra came out of my profound spiritual maturity, but the truth was I'd learned that there are some situations you don't want to ever have to go back into. And my spiritual path required me to keep my side of the street clean no matter what. I didn't want to have to go back and say I'm sorry to anyone in that building. I raised the spatula anyway.

"No," I said to the man who cared more about where we parked than my pain.

"I didn't read the lease this morning before I came to cart my life away. It came up pretty fast, my marriage dissolving. I didn't think about the elevator." Tears started to fall silently and would not stop. I held myself back from swatting him with the spatula like the fly he was in an already miserable day. What I really wanted to do was punch him. "We're splitting up," I said. "I'm leaving, she's staying. I'll be out of here before you know it."

Luckily for me, my friends saw the scene unfolding and circled in close. They put me in the car and made sure I buckled my seat belt as life as I knew it dissolved like salt in water: tears falling, snot flying, grip tight on that spatula. I continued to hold onto some inner resolve that all would not be lost as we lined my new bedroom with boxes.

The move-out went as well as it could go. Trying to be helpful, my ex-wife had boxed things up for me, made choices with and without me about who got what. Ten-plus years of sheets and towels and knick-knacks were neatly stacked and packed, each item a carrier of memories I would now hold alone. Perhaps she did it out of kindness, perhaps she just wanted us to get in and quickly out of what was now her space. I don't know exactly why she packed everything up like that, but I do know how it felt.

Seeing all those neatly stacked packages full of what used to be our shared life, I felt boxed up, discarded, and dismissed.

You never know what will push you over the edge. For me, it's always a seemingly small thing. Something happens—some song or word or look or thing takes you by surprise and it's suddenly all too much when just a moment ago you were busy competently handling a crisis. With my divorce, that small thing was the spatula.

I found myself flashing back in time, standing in the kitchen store weeks before our wedding, choosing registry items, and I was fighting for these particular pots and pans to make it onto the list. They'd last forever if we took good care of them, if I used the right utensils, like the spatula, an investment in a lifetime of holidays and breakfasts.

Standing there in the apartment we once shared five years later, I wondered—how could she pack up the pots and pans for me to take, the ones meant to last a lifetime, and leave out the spatula?

Even in that moment of pain, I knew that the missing spatula wasn't some intentional act of spite. Logic told me there was no larger message in the absence of this ten-dollar kitchen tool. Still, the emotions roared through me, surprising me with their force as I stood outside in the driveway and watched my friends heave the last of the remnants of our life together into the borrowed pickup truck.

Years later, friends would say to me, Remember the spatula? Remember how you almost punched that guy? How you held on to that utensil for days? I'd tell this story back to them: I remember how you circled round, how you let me fall apart. I remember how you lifted those boxes and hauled what I had and tucked me in on the couch when I had nowhere else to go. That's what I remember.

White-knuckling that spatula became a symbol in my life, a physical representation of the inner grip it takes sometimes to survive—a reminder that I still had some control over what I would bring along and what I would let go, what I would take, and what I would leave behind. Even when someone else presented me with everything they thought I needed, all taped up and labeled in boxes I did not want. Somehow that spatula meant I still had choices.

I could choose whether to punch that guy or not, what amends I could bear to let myself earn and make later.

I could choose to call my friends for help, to accept the gift of their help.

I could say yes to my roommate that first Christmas, when all I wanted to do was cry, and join her on a midnight drive to see the lights, celebratory Burger King crowns perched on our heads.

I could choose what words I would use, and I could say yes to the spark that fired in my heart when a woman I'd watched from across a crowded room sent me a real old-time letter. I could put the pen in my hand even when my heart was in my throat and risk loving again.

Something about that spatula meant I could choose to laugh at myself even in the midst of the pain.

Twenty years later, another loss came my way when our house caught on fire. My spiritual director gave me some uncharacteristically direct advice. "Don't try to make sense of this for at least two years," she said. "You need to let this unfold before you can know what it will mean for you."

With the wounds healed over and the scars secure, looking back on that day in the driveway with the gift of time, I could see an unfolding: The nosy neighbor. The taped-up boxes. The pickup truck. I could choose again what to take and what to leave behind. But this time it wouldn't be about which knickknack or kitchen utensil to hold on to. This time I could choose what story to tell, what lesson to learn, and what love to remember.

My first wife and I had been college sweethearts, growing up together into adulthood in a world that actively despised us. Women who loved women. Women who questioned the culture that tried to consume us. Women who bucked the norms of gender and society. Smart and serious. Together for ten years, neither of us expected it to end.

I loved her deeply. We were keepers of each other's stories. Sharers of kindness. Care. Passion. Healing. Family. Even with all of my sadness and anger, even with all that I left behind, there was a lot I wanted to keep.

It was her parents who made sure I had a winter coat when seminary began, knowing that if I had to lead a graveside service, I needed something other than mismatched layers. It was her family that brought this paycheck-to-paycheck girl to Europe, teaching me the joy of cinnamon sugar roasted nuts at the Christkindlmarkt and what to eat at their village pub where, yes, that really was beef-flavored jello with hard-boiled eggs and vegetables floating in it. It was her family that welcomed me in and held on to me as their own until it was time to let me go. I wanted to keep the experience of that love, that care, that opening of the world, even if I couldn't keep them.

Same-sex marriage was a far-off, not-in-my-life-time dream when we stood before our family and friends inside the walls of our church and promised to love each other today, tomorrow, and forever. There were no legal requirements, no protections or ramifications to our vows. We created our own rituals.

When we got married, we chose a new name. A shared last name, a family name, something permanent. We filled out the paperwork and went before the judge. I kept the name. And years later, when that relationship ended, I took the spatula, too.

I've chosen to let go of a lot of things.

I've let go of the idea that that marriage's ending was solely my fault.

I've let go of the idea that I failed.

I've stopped hiding the fact that I've been married and divorced. That the name I carry was never mine alone but began as ours.

I've let go of the self-judgment, let go of the anger.

I choose to keep the love—love from her and from her family and our friends and that church that aligned itself with us when it could have turned away.

I choose to remember that we can make our own markers, write our own rituals, make our own way even in a world that would rather have us dead.

I choose to keep and to tell the stories of those friends who circled round, who carried the mattress in from the curb and kept the nosy neighbor at bay, the ones who opened their home and tucked me in on their couch, the one who looked at me months later, when I told her about a girl I was writing those letters to—how I couldn't eat or get my heartbeat to slow down—the way she looked at me and said "Sounds like love," when I never thought I'd love again.

Sorting and sifting, I choose the life-giving, life-saving, heart-expanding, whole-story-telling truth. I don't wipe away the suffering. Grief and gratitude can live side by side.

My heart still aches sometimes, wondering what might have been even though I want nothing more than exactly what I have now. But no one ever really leaves us, or us them. As a wise one in my life says, the part of me that belongs to you is always with you, and the part of you that belongs to me is always with me, no matter whether we are physically with each other or not. That's just how it is.

All these years later, I can tell the story a new way. Choosing my language carefully, I can decide to keep the kindness, the love, the feeling of family. I can remember the defiance we felt, determined that other people's hatred would not destroy us. I can live my life, content with my own sense of wholeness and joy.

Nearly twenty years later, I know something I didn't know that day in the driveway. That what I took taped up in all those neatly labeled boxes wasn't final. Other people could try to tidy up my experiences and fit them into a shape that worked for them, but it was up to me to choose what meaning I'd make of the events that came my way.

As a minister, I get the honor of holding so many people's stories. I've learned that everybody suffers, and that much of our suffering comes from the stories we tell ourselves and others. When we listen too much to what others think about our lives, when we fall into old traps of assigning meaning to random events, when we focus our attention on the fire and forget the people standing right in front of us with hands extended, the stories of suffering are telling us.

Yet when we pause long enough to listen and get curious enough to question, we can shift the story in life-giving ways.

Sometimes I try to imagine I'm telling the story of someone else's life. I'm so much kinder to them. So much more forgiving with the time it takes them to learn the lessons and recover from the sorrows. So much more hopeful about the outcome. Maybe that's one of the ways we can wiggle ourselves free from some of the suffering. We can imagine the kids are listening in or someone else we love is in need of a little kindness. How would we tell the story then? What would we leave out, and where would we focus in?

Chapter 3

Take That

Getting to know who we are isn't always the easiest assignment. All of us are shaped by the voices of our families, our cultures, and our society. All of us have parts of our histories that have gone unhealed, or habits that have to stop. Maybe we have genetic predispositions we'd prefer to ignore, or a series of circumstances has left us in a hole financially. These things we struggle with may not always feel as threatening as a house on fire, but the damage from these unattended harms can go way beyond a lost home. For me, all that unhealed history showed up in alcoholism.

I knew from an early age that I drank differently from the people around me. Not everyone headed to the basement when they got off the bus from middle school and mixed themselves a drink from their parents' bar, but I did. I was fourteen when the diagnosis became official.

A psychiatrist I'd seen one time sent me to the hospital. Apparently, it also wasn't typical to want to die all the time. I didn't know that.

My time in the hospital turned out to be a gift. A safe place. Some acknowledgment that everything was not, in fact, okay. People who could see the depth of my pain, pay attention just to me, and help figure out what would keep me alive. I didn't want to talk about anything, but part of me was glad to be there.

A few days into my hospitalization, the school district sent a tutor. They brought mind-numbing worksheets well below my grade level. Somehow my math teacher got wind of this. Unacceptable, she declared. With no tutors available who could teach me my French and chemistry and math assignments, she devised her own plan. She conscripted the best and brightest of my classmates and sent them to the hospital each night. On good days, I'd get a pass to go sit in the lobby with them, conjugating verbs and reviewing formulas, and on bad days, my classmates would meet me upstairs, passing first through the locked doors, then the search and screening, and finally into a tiny room, table and chairs bolted to the ground, where I waited.

We didn't exactly run in the same crowd, these kids and I, and truth be told I wasn't particularly happy to see them. I imagined them—these goody-two-shoes of my high school traveling not to France with the choir but to this foreign land of misery and sorrow each night—full of condescension and unwanted sympathy.

In fact, I took very real pleasure in freaking them out. "Someone tried to kill themselves with a plastic fork this morning," I'd say as they tentatively opened our advanced algebra books. Fuck you, I thought, pushing them away whatever their intentions.

Much later I saw these students as a lifeline. Each of them in their neat Tretorn tennis shoes and collar-up Izod shirts. Each of them a messenger from a teacher who refused to give up on me.

As the limit of our insurance neared, the doctor presented me with a choice: transfer to the state hospital, where I would stay indefinitely, or go back home and follow the rules he laid out for me. I knew about the state hospital. It was the end of the road. My teacher and my classmates could not follow me there. College, the long dreamed-for way out, would disappear.

I signed on to the ridiculous rules. Random drug and alcohol testing anytime my parents picked.

A grade average of B or better. Weekly therapy sessions and no more arguing about taking the antidepressants as prescribed. All of this in exchange for the chance to come home with no curfew and no rules and a room of my own in the basement.

From the outside, these rules probably seemed more than reasonable given the trouble I had gotten in. But sometimes the rules that seem so reasonable for other people don't quite fit for you or for me. Sometimes we have to find our own way.

Sometimes what you take is a chance.

Going home meant reentry into school and a visit with the principal, a woman I actively despised. She'd chased me across the parking lot, yelled at me down the hallway, and snuck up on me as I hid behind the dumpster trying to sneak a cigarette or a drink between classes. We didn't talk. You could say she yelled and I ran. I considered her evil.

As I sat in her office, she suggested that I come back to school part-time, half days, and consider dropping my more challenging classes. Maybe that would help me feel less overwhelmed as I made this big transition. She wanted me to succeed, she said. What I heard was condescension. What I heard her say was I couldn't do it. Sitting there in her tidy office, her in her purple suit, I faced her in my ripped jeans and rolled-up bandannas wrapped around my wrists to hide my scars. Welling up in me was the forceful *fuck you* that has saved my life again and again.

"No," I told her. "I'm coming back. Full-time, same classes. People have been investing in me, and I'm not going to let them down."

Thirty years later, I wonder if the principal I assumed was a moron knew exactly what she was doing. Maybe she actually did want me to succeed. And maybe she saw the fight in me and added fuel to the fire that saved me. Whatever her intentions, I went back to school and got to work.

A year later, I found her in the lunchroom and shoved a piece of paper into her hands. *Accepted*, I showed her. Early decision. Smith College. Full ride. *Fuck you*.

I don't remember her reaction. She's more of a mythical figure than an actual person to me. She represented authority, boundaries, someone telling me what I could and couldn't do. In my imagination, she became someone who wanted me to fail—even though that was likely the furthest thing from her mind.

Whatever her intention, I recreated her as useful fuel, a person who thought I couldn't do it. My opposition propelling me out of that place like a rocket.

Fuck you, I'd mutter as I studied late into the night. *Fuck you*, I said as I finished my college essay. *Fuck you*, I'd sputter, fueled by anger and rage, living in the tunnel of my own mind, my own fears and hopes and longings.

At the time I didn't know the fancy words to describe what I was experiencing or what I was pushing back against. I didn't know that this pushing was part of my identity. The language would come later, but the propelling impulse was clear. This fight in me was the will to survive, to live outside of the boxes I felt trapped inside by the family and systems and culture I landed within.

I wanted out. And the animal instinct that lived in me—the spark of the divine within fighting for life—was fighting like hell to survive.

That blessed fuck-you attitude kept me alive as I pushed back on bullshit expectations and ridiculous rules that were meant for somebody else. But it also kept me from connecting. Kept me from accurately seeing myself and the world around me. The anger that fueled me kept me far from other people and far from those untended places in myself that needed healing.

James Baldwin once wrote, "one of the reasons people cling to their hates so stubbornly is because they sense that once hate is gone, they will be forced to deal with pain." In his writing about race in America, he brought insight to a fundamental defense mechanism of human nature: we push away pain with anger when we fear the pain beneath.

It took several more years for sobriety to take hold for me. Having someone else tell me that I needed to stop drinking when they had no understanding of the pain I carried wouldn't do it. I had to have something I cared about losing, and that something was the life I had started to build away from my family, away from the home that had always owned me.

I was twenty-two when sobriety finally stuck. Two hospitalizations, a handful of therapists, and some wise friends finally did the trick. They introduced me to recovery, and I grabbed on with a willingness I hadn't previously known. This was *my* life I was going to lose if I didn't face this difficult truth about myself. Welling up in me was a forceful FU— and I hope you'll pardon the raw language (again), but the rawness and anger of the two-word phrase were precisely what made it necessary for me, allowing me to assert myself, pushing me to save my own life over and over again. If I was going to make it, I needed to find a way to respond to the world that went beyond *fuck you*.

It helped that I found someone funny, kind, and supportive to guide me through. One of the first assignments I got in sobriety went like this:

> "Go to the ice cream shop down the street and try a different flavor every day. You've been numbed out for so long you don't even know what you like.
>
> "Try them all, one flavor at a time," she told me. "Figure out if you like vanilla or chocolate, strawberry or peppermint. Do you want your ice cream with nuts on top? How about chocolate whipped cream? What do you like? Get curious and go find out who you are."

In service to my health, this was clearly one of the best assignments of all time. I needed to eat ice cream. All of the ice cream.

Now I know that this is not the right assignment for everyone, especially if you struggle with sugar addiction, but for me at the time it was absolutely the right assignment. So much of the work of recovery felt impossible to me. Day after day I walked into church basements and community centers to talk to strangers about my feelings—ugh!—all without the numbing effect of alcohol. This was definitely not fun.

Eating ice cream, figuring out what I liked (and so discovering some long-hidden aspects of who I was), sharing this experiment with others as we sat on the wall in the sun outside the ice cream shop laughing and gagging over Butter Brickle—that was fun. If this was what recovery felt like, maybe I could keep going a little bit longer.

When I entered my second year of sobriety, the people supporting me let me in on another piece of information. You're going to start experiencing a bigger range of emotions now, they told me. It won't just be happy or angry or sad. Sometimes it will be happy and angry and sad at the same time. It's all part of growing up emotionally.

Now when my nine-year-old daughter explains what it's like inside her body as we wait in line for the roller-coaster, butterflies in her stomach that tell her she is excited and nervous all at the same time, I listen, amazed at what she knows about herself and her emotional life. A multiplicity of emotions all in the same moment—something I am still learning to feel and trust. There is more than one way of experiencing and understanding any given story of our life unfolding right now, and more than one way to understand the story behind us, too.

My therapist has been teaching me to move beyond the either/or mindset I've clung to, to learn the concept of both/and—where multiple things can be true all at the same time. Among the first complexities I learned was that people can love you *and* hurt you. You can understand things one way now and another way later and both are true. We can be in the same room, objectively witnessing the same events, and experience them completely differently. Your culture and mine, our backgrounds, life experiences, opportunities, worldviews, identities, and so much more shift and change, a kaleidoscope of possibility and beauty. There is so much more fullness than just *fuck you*.

Now that kaleidoscopic lens helps me see other possibilities differently.

Maybe, just maybe, that principal with the PhD and all the awards was, in fact, trying to help me.

Maybe the students who came to teach me in the hospital and the teacher who sent them made the effort to keep me tethered to the best parts of myself, seeing education as a lifeline out of an untenable situation.

Maybe love was always there, right alongside the pain.

All of us have the potential to turn the kaleidoscope this way or that. To see new pieces of a story emerge, the light and color shifting in ways that ultimately rework the design.

At twenty-two I didn't know that anything aside from *fuck you* could save me. Didn't know I could feel more than one emotion at a time, didn't know that people would love and care for me in ways that would bring me back to myself, healed and healing. I didn't even know what kind of ice cream I liked!

When we open ourselves to multiple interpretations of our stories, the stories we've told and been told start to own us less and less. We become more flexible and open, more curious and less judgmental. Maybe a little kindness for ourselves could even move in beside the pain. A little grief beside the gratitude. Like my nine-year-old daughter, we *can* feel anger and excitement, nervousness and joy all at the same time. Letting in new light, we turn the wheel of the kaleidoscope, looking out at the beautiful complexity all around us, approaching, I imagine, what it might be like to see with god's eyes—feeling and knowing all of what is true at the same time and holding all of it, and each of us, with love.

Chapter 4

Take Off

Most folks in the helping professions agree that running away from your feelings is bad, but that might not always be true. Of course, resentments rotting your guts isn't a great choice, and okay, it's better not to sit on your sadness until it sits on you and you can't get out of bed. And that traumatic experience is less likely to rule your life with some air and light around it. But seriously, isn't there anything else we can do?

In a book handed out with frequency to people new to sobriety, there's a hint of that anything else. First published in the 1970s, *Living Sober* has been printed over fifty times since then. Though the content is now dated, its central purpose is clear. *Living Sober* is about, well, *living* sober. It's about what to do in all those days after you put down the drink. In some ways, it's about every life change where you face a dramatic moment, make the decision, and take the turn into a new way of being. And it's about the whole rest of your life waiting for you out there on the terrifying horizon of each day.

Even though everyone tells you to take it one day at a time—and thinking about it that way does help—something inside you knows that if this life change is going to stick, it means changing your behavior forever, with each day bringing a new set of challenges.

Somewhere around day thirty of my sobriety, someone handed me a copy of *Living Sober*. Thirty-one practical tips and suggestions on how to stay away from a drink, redirect your thinking, and live sober in the hopefully countless days you will go on to live in recovery. At the time I had no interest in talking about my feelings constantly. Heck, I didn't even know what they were half the time. What I needed was something to do. This book was perfect for me.

I made my way through it, trying each suggestion one at a time. It wasn't as much fun as trying all those different flavors of ice cream, but the methodical approach and techniques and the spirit of discovery stuck. Reading through the book, trying each tip, I starred the ones that worked—and left the rest behind. Something in me knew that I'd be using that book like a lifeline when the urge to drink dropped in, and I'd need to be able to do a fast scan to find relief.

I wasn't a huge fan of #10, "Making use of 'telephone therapy,'" also known as calling a friend. I hated #16, "Being good to yourself," and #12, "Getting plenty of rest," was never going to happen. But #9, "Eating or drinking something—usually, sweet," and #6, "Getting active," seemed like possibilities.

Once I got to the end of the book, I filled the remaining blank pages with my own tricks and tips, growing the list of suggestions I could turn to whenever I felt myself wanting a drink or going to the less helpful places in my mind. I added simple stuff like taking a bath—because naked and wet, I was a whole lot less likely to head out to the liquor store. I added tater tots, because those almost always took the edge off. Planning my next tattoo, making a cup of tea, and calling it a day and going to bed early all made the list. And when it was really, really bad, I'd hop in my car and take off.

When I bought my first car, I was fourteen. A 1971 pea-green Chevy Nova with rusted-out floors, a car we had to push up the driveway. I couldn't get my license until I turned sixteen, but so what? At $300, the car was a steal, and I told myself I'd have a year and a half to learn how to fix it. I ran my hand over its hood every time I walked in and out our door, imagining freedom and escape.

When my father taught me how to clean a carburetor, scrape away the rust, attach the wire mesh, apply the fiberglass, and sand it all down to prime and paint, I listened. I learned about the end of leaded gas and how to read a repair manual found in the library stacks. I learned to hold my tongue as my father swore, handing him the pliers or the wrench, containing my sense of injustice and the rank sarcasm that coursed through my teenage mind as he did what I could not: work magic on that car. I'd cool down imagining the wind in my hair, flying down the highway with the windows rolled down and the music blasting.

Even with all of our attention and care, my pea-green Chevy Nova rarely left the driveway. The repair list only seemed to grow as we worked. The guy down the street had a beauty to sell. This time, for $1,000, I got a 1968 straight-six cherry-red, black-top Chevy II Nova—a muscle car, revved up and ready to go. Sure, the front bench seat only attached to the floor on one side, so you'd slide and swerve when you took the corners. Yes, it did stall out every time you went through a puddle, the questionable electric system shorting out at the worst possible moments. And yes, it was fast and loud and when you hit the gas it took your breath away. That car turned heads, and every day I drove it I could hardly believe it was mine.

Once I had my license I'd drive downtown to the city in the afternoons, weaving through the streets of Baltimore, making my way to my internship at the lab where we studied the effects of hypoxia on neonatal rat brain astrocytes—surely that would look good on my college application. At night, I'd drive to work at Wendy's or the pizza shop, and on weekends, I'd open up the engine, tearing down Route 40 until I could head off the highway, weaving my way down the back roads to the retreat center where I'd go with my church youth group.

Each time I'd take the turn onto the property, my breath would get deeper, the dust of the dirt road swirling up behind my bright red car as I eased in to park by the old brick buildings. I'd sit by the pond, careful to avoid the aggressive geese. I'd walk down the road where the tractors rolled by and visit the cows, wondering if the electric fence was live or not that day. Sometimes someone came out from one of the buildings to talk to me, but most of the time I was alone. That retreat center was a place of safety and rest for me. A place where I could be seen and not seen all at the same time. The push-pull of loneliness and longing letting up enough that I could slow down and breathe. If god was anywhere, I thought, god was there.

At seventeen, I graduated from high school and took a summer job at that retreat center. Fifty hours of work bought me a bed and a hundred dollars a week. Space to breathe, work hard, help others, and think less about myself. I packed up my muscle car and took off. I didn't know then that I was moving out of my parents' house forever. I did know that I needed a fresh start, and I took it. I needed to figure out who I was away from my family, our history, and my actions. I needed room to recover who I was outside the influence of our family system. I needed to be released from the grip of who I had been if I was going to discover the person I wanted to be.

When I was twenty-two, I let go of my muscle car. I got a respectable job in my field after graduation from college, and driving was part of it. Every afternoon, I picked up and dropped off kids who were part of my program. Kids who lived with mental health challenges and disrupted homes. Kids who definitely didn't need the extra excitement of having my car crap out in the middle of a puddle or a blizzard. One day, after the windshield wipers and the heat both failed in the middle of an ice storm, I walked into the local car dealer and traded it in—traded that 1968 cherry-red, black-top muscle car for a used Toyota Corolla. The ultimate responsible car.

At least it was red.

The reality was that my life was changing. On the outside, I was starting to look a lot more like everybody else. I let my hair grow out from the mandatory coming-out flattop of college to a bob. I traded my leather jacket and boots for fleece and flannel, polo shirts and khaki pants. The life of stability and structure I'd longed for was taking shape.

This summer, I'll mark a milestone: nine years in one house, one city, one job—the longest I've stayed put with no plans to move since I left home at seventeen.

I still like to take off, though. Only now it's in a Subaru.

Every summer, my kids and I hit the road, traveling by car all over the country. We started this ritual when the kids were two and five, and by now, we have a well-worn rhythm, logging at least three thousand miles each July. I love planning these trips—finding the quirky roadside stops, the small towns with unknown treasures, mapping out a few known destinations and a whole lot of space in between. I love knowing that for a minimum of a month, everything we need is in that car. One small suitcase and a backpack apiece. No fancy Sunday clothes or staff meetings to run, no one from school or church to find us, just a shit ton of sunscreen and first-aid supplies. Taking off means shaking it all off, letting all of that pretense and practicality fall away.

"Taking off" is one of my additions to *Living Sober*. I'm still not always a fan of talking things out, but tea, tater tots, open roads, new horizons, smashing stuff, sanding and priming, hard work, helping others— these are all on my list. *Living Sober* was a good place to start for me. But the blank space at the end of the book to add my own ideas has been even better.

Chapter 5

Turns Out You Take It All with You

Sometimes other people's stories help us to better understand our own. Maybe that's why I've always been a voracious reader. Safely snuggled in on my couch, I can travel the world, immersing myself in history or science or fantasy. No smelly strangers or food I don't want to try, no uncomfortable silences as I get to know new people. Just me and my book and the adventure unfolding at a pace I can control.

Specialists in trauma will tell you that folks who have experienced a lot of uncertainty and loss are often less likely to approach the unknown with curiosity. New people, places, and ideas can be stress-provoking. Most of us can understand this when we consider what we are drawn to in times of crisis—comfort food, the stuffed animal from childhood, the blanket or coffee or sounds and smells from our safe place. Curiosity and exploration can and do happen for folks who have experienced trauma, but it helps if they happen at a pace the person can choose. For me, reading offered that perfect element of control.

Reading wasn't only about the far away; it was also about understanding the very near. Growing up, I read my way through the psychology section of our local library as if my life depended on it. As I observed my mother's erratic and scary behavior, I wanted to understand what was happening with her—and what I could do to help. Gathering up all of the information I could find helped me feel less out of control, as the science showed more compassion than society, naming mental illness as just that—an illness—instead of a moral failing. The stories and the science I encountered in those books softened my heart and shifted my understanding, opening up the possibility that my mother's inconsistent ability to care for us might not be my fault and might not be in my power to control or cure. As important as those experiences of her illness were for me as a child, once I left home I knew I would have my own life to live, my own story to write. All those books helped me understand not only her but myself.

When I graduated from high school, my grandparents presented me with a matching set of luggage. Immigrants at the end of World War II, they knew what it was like to arrive in a new country with only what they could carry, their shipping crates turned into coffee tables, their passage into a new life their most secure possession. My grandfather had been a prisoner of war, my grandmother left alone to survive the repeated bombing of London. Their firstborn son arrived and perished without ever meeting his father. Searching for a fresh start away from the war-torn ruins of their past, my grandparents moved to the United States. They arrived into the embrace of my grandmother's sister, who prepared a path for them. For my grandparents, travel symbolized new beginnings, and their gift of luggage signaled their hopes and dreams of a new future for me.

Somehow they knew that I, too, had lived in a kind of war-torn land. That something wasn't right at home and this chance at college could be my one-way ticket across the ocean of despair. Graduating from high school and heading off to college was a big deal, and I remember receiving this extravagant gift from them and feeling both excited and a little confused.

I did not know about all of these bags. Why were they different sizes, and what were they for? I recognized the duffel bag, and I could tell that one suitcase was big and one was small, though I didn't yet know why. The concept of a carry-on bag was well beyond my experience. But the one that really confounded me was the garment bag. What was that, with all of its hooks and latches and pockets? Why did it fold in half, and who had enough dress clothes to fill a bag like that, anyway? Then someone told me what it was for, and I began to dream of the day I'd be jetting off to a job interview in California and I'd need to travel light. Just my interview clothes and a nice pair of shoes tucked neatly into my new garment bag.

In the meantime, I packed up every piece of that luggage for my arrival at college. I didn't know yet just how important it would feel to try to look the part as I arrived at an elite New England women's college. On the outside, I did my best to fit in. On the inside, I felt much more comfortable washing dishes and cutting up fruit for catering trays in the kitchen, heading out the back door by the dumpster with the chefs for a smoke.

My first African American history course revealed the tip of the iceberg of what I did not know about the history of my country. So much had been left out—so many stories of so many people left behind. My introduction to world religions class taught me that most scholars believed the Bible had multiple authors, that the church had done horrible things in pursuit of power, and that there were other ways beyond Christianity to rightly orient your life. I fell into poetry and was caught by Audre Lorde and Adrienne Rich. I took theater and psychology classes—so many psychology classes. It felt overwhelming, all of this new information coming at me at once, opening up new vistas of possibility about how to understand this world and my life.

My first-year college roommate was outgoing and funny and kind. Our mutual love of the Grateful Dead was enough to match us up in the housing lottery and get us off to a strong start. One Friday night we did what all first-year students at our women's college did at some point: we took the bus to the nearby coed college to attend a party. I didn't know anyone there, and I didn't really know how to get home, but we stuck together and it seemed okay. My roommate met up with an old friend from high school, and he came back to spend the night in our room. I didn't think anything of it. We were all drunk, and he was a friend. What could go wrong?

Being passed out in the corner, I wouldn't know until the next day that this old friend raped my roommate.

I'm sure she heard the voices in her head that get put there from birth in America. If you let someone into your home, if you let someone into your bed, if you are drunk, if you kissed them, if you did this or they did that—then the other person's forcing themselves on you cannot count as rape. There are so many ways culture blames the victim, letting the one who did the hurting off the hook while you yourself are hanged on it. Sometimes you just keep your mouth shut and live in your shame because it seems easier than speaking.

I hope my roommate encountered more honest and loving voices than the ones screaming in my head. I wish I could say that I responded with the loving and empowering words my forty-something self would say now, but I don't remember my response. I do remember that she requested a room change. And before I knew it, she was gone, and I was left alone.

Watching my roommate's story unfold in front of me started to shift how I understood my own. If what happened to her counted as rape, and it certainly did, then what would you call what happened to me?

I brought my story and my questions to the counseling center. One memory led to another and another. With the help of a counselor, I began naming and renaming the experiences as I understood them anew. Categories shifted. What I thought was normal was not. What I once named as my fault was a more complicated picture. Secrets and shame started to see the light of day.

Trying to understand what was happening to me, I turned again to books. I learned about post-traumatic stress disorder and our survival responses—the way that our bodies are hardwired to go into fight-or-flight mode when confronted with a threat. Attempts to escape are considered the flight response, and attempts to win whatever battle is in front of us are considered the fight response. In time, other ways of responding to trauma would be validated, too, shifting my understanding again. But in that moment, in 1992, when Judith Herman's *Trauma and Recovery* served as both a lifeline and a textbook in my life, the understanding of fight and flight as responses to trauma helped me to see myself and the ways I coped with newfound compassion. College was my ultimate fight and flight, a combination of fuck you and hitting the road—I was trying to simultaneously escape and beat the odds, fighting against the culture and the life events that could have constrained me.

Many years later, I learned about some of the other ways a body responds to trauma, and my understanding shifted again. In addition to fight and flight, some bodies cope with trauma by freezing. When your brain believes you are in life-threatening danger without any way to escape or fend off the attack, your body might respond this way. This can be literal, like when you can't turn the wheel even though you see the oncoming car heading your way in traffic or you can't imagine another option when your partner comes at you with another string of emotionally or physically abusive actions. People who experience this freeze response to trauma talk about it as feeling disconnected, numb, or shut down. In an action-oriented society where we are obsessed with the illusion of pulling ourselves up by our own bootstraps, the freeze response can feel especially shameful even though it is just as natural and protective as fighting. For folks who have experienced long-lasting trauma, unfreezing and beginning to feel and move and reconnect to their emotions and their bodies can be lifelong work.

There alone in my suddenly single room at college, I began to unfreeze. Sunlight was streaming in in earnest. The ice was beginning to thaw. The locked-in ways of my life were loosening up. As I started to understand the events of my life in new ways, I also began to understand the facts of the world in new ways. Curiosity and exploration took hold as I learned new facts, made new associations, and began to write new stories.

Somehow, though, I was still stuck. The therapist I was seeing dropped a bomb to try and dislodge me: "I can't help you heal any more unless you stop drinking. You're not going to get better until you put down the alcohol."

Fuck you. Flight was my response to this traumatic concept. I stomped out of her office. She didn't know how much I hurt. And was she like every therapist in the world who thought people were better off not drinking? Clearly this was some kind of therapist conspiracy.

But slowly her words sunk in. I had not come all this way to get sucked back into that vortex of pain. I had escaped—the flight and fight in me had worked—and still the trauma had come with me. If I wanted to get better, if I wanted to feel less pain on a daily basis, I was going to have to let go of the things that numbed me out, and the unfreezing was going to hurt like hell.

I put down the drink. Took myself to recovery meetings and sat in the back with my arms crossed against my black-leather-jacket-clad chest. I felt like I was drowning. I stopped sleeping and started cutting myself again—a habit I'd stopped when I was fourteen. Thoughts of suicide visited me every day, an imagined way out when it all felt like too much. After several months of this, with symptoms worsening, my therapist suggested a trip to the hospital. I went. And it felt like defeat, even with people around me promising it was a way to keep fighting.

Signing myself in was saying yes to life—even if it didn't feel that way at the time. There in the hospital I had a chance to stabilize and stay safe. Several weeks later, when it was time to return to school, I kept the story of where I'd been to myself, scared of the stigma that came with a psychiatric hospitalization. The hospital I'd slipped away to handily named itself the Retreat, so if anyone asked, that's where I'd been—"on retreat" in the middle of the semester. When I returned, I realized the college had filled the vacant space in my room. I had a new roommate.

Meeting her on that first day, suitcases in hand, I felt terrified. I worried that this hospitalization signaled the start of a pattern, and that from now on I'd be in and out of crisis for the rest of my life. I worried she would show pity or disgust. I worried about needing help to stay on track, and I knew what I needed for support, but I didn't know if I could ask for it.

These were just a few of the story lines going through my mind when I met my new roommate. Walking into the room we now shared, I dropped my bags and decided to go for it. She'd find out sooner or later; I might as well tell the truth. I told her where I'd been and why. I told her that I was newly sober and it would help if we didn't have any alcohol or drugs in the room. I told her that I had a hard time sleeping and needed the lights on all the time. I told her that I might be sad or anxious sometimes and that she didn't need to fix it, but she should know I couldn't always make it better. I told her that I'd understand if she wanted to request a move to a different room. And then I shut up and waited for the onslaught of her response.

What she said was, "Okay. Thanks for telling me. We can keep the lights on and keep this a sober space.

You were so brave to go get the help you needed. Let me know if there's anything I can do to make things easier."

From there, we talked about our favorite bands and which classes were harder and how to make ten-cent ramen taste better. That's how I returned to school, shocked at the casual kindness of this stranger who showed me another possibility, countering the stigma I feared with a well-lighted room.

This single moment shifted something for me. Because it was so simple, so everyday, and so different from what I expected, I could almost hear the change happen. Her straightforward, accepting response showed me that people do really exist who can hear the truth about the pain and the challenges so many of us carry without running away or thinking less of us.

Her response was something I recognized much later, as I read the words of Dr. Clarissa Pinkola Estés, who wrote, "Ours is not the task of fixing the entire world all at once, but of stretching out to mend the part of the world that is within our reach. Any small, calm thing that one soul can do to help another soul, to assist some portion of this poor suffering world, will help immensely."

My roommate's small, calm words soothed my soul.

This was not the end of my struggles, but it was a beginning. The beginning of me telling the truth and being met with connection and love instead of fear.

I paid attention to my roommate's responses over the rest of the year, as she taught me to reach for something new. She lived with abandon, working and playing hard, laughing louder than anyone I knew. She had big feelings—sadness and rage and joy—and she expressed them all. And she had friendships that held firm through all kinds of ups and downs. She lived large for someone so small.

Watching her, I wanted what she had. I noticed that my range of emotions was nowhere near as large as hers. I longed to feel more than pain, to be more than numb. I wanted joy and laughter and satisfaction. Yes, part of me was still frozen, but I was beginning to thaw, and I wanted to know what it felt like to be all the way alive.

For those of us who have faced that despair, who for too long have been fighting and flying and freezing, there comes a time when we know we can no longer outrun the repeating images in our head or the clutching fear in our heart. New luggage, a new job, a new school, a new partner, new friends, a new place—none of it completely cures the pain or reverses the coping mechanisms we carry in our bodies. There comes a time when we know we can't outrun it anymore. I knew that the time was up for me. I had tried fight and flight. Now it was time to unfreeze.

I went in sideways (according to character) and saw that brought me the most success. I discovered other people's stories of survival, I read other people's poetry, I consumed manifestos of the marginalized, I imagined futures of collective liberation—and each of these filled me with hope.

Cherríe Moraga. Toni Cade Bambara. Sylvia Plath, Emily Dickinson, Anne Sexton. Ntozake Shange. Adrienne Rich. Mary Oliver, Audre Lorde.

I read them all, their stories helping me better understand my own. Their words warming me, capturing the full range of emotion I longed for. I began to imagine a future that held it all.

Reading let me move in sideways to a sense of wholeness, to enter foreign landscapes that could inform my own. I found Audre Lorde's poem "A Litany for Survival" and Mary Oliver's "The Journey." Their stories told me I was not alone. We were survivors, reaching beyond our painful experiences and writing whole poems, crafting whole lives from the resilience and wreckage. Their words kept me company on many a bathroom floor as I put down the drink and let the ice that had encased me thaw.

For years I had hidden how I felt, kept my secrets tucked deep inside—and here were these nationally renowned poets telling the whole wide world how they felt and what they knew. Silence had not saved them, and it would not save me. And even though talking about my feelings would never be my favorite way of handling things, I needed to speak.

I started speaking slowly, finding trustworthy people, building up my community. As I healed, I learned there were other ways to respond to trauma, too. Ways that went beyond fight or flight or freeze. I learned that trauma included more than wartime experiences and women's responses to sexual assault, that the incessant everyday nature of micro- and macroaggressions experienced by people of color in America, by trans folx and queer folx, immigrants, people with disabilities, youth, elders, women, and so many others—can all add up to a weathering effect of trauma. I learned that one way people cope with trauma is to tend their communities, turning their attention to the things they can change, building each other up, and taking back control where they can to improve conditions for others.

I learned that helping others soothed more than just me.

Those young adult years were all about creating a new sober family full of misfits who kept each other safe and smiling, shifting my story from outcast solo survivor to one among many who lifted each other up. Sure, I was terrified and broke and sad at times, but I had people who would sit with me even when I could not speak. People who took me to the batting cage or the driving range, who piled up ten-cent dishes from the Goodwill and smashed them with me in the alley when the feelings got to be too much and my body needed to be put into motion, with sound and company and ritual. Far from home, I sometimes felt guilty for surviving, for leaving my mother and my brother and my father behind to cope with the challenges that remained. With Audre Lorde's words and so many others' ringing in my ears, I remembered that my silence would not save me. Telling my story and speaking out would ultimately serve not just me—it would also support my collective, my new family of misfits, to go beyond surviving to thriving.

I continued to study psychology, to read in books to understand what I knew loosely from life. I learned about bipolar disorder and other serious, persistent mental illnesses. I learned about positive and negative and intermittent reinforcement—how the possibility that something good might come from a behavior could keep a person coming back to a nearly dry well forever. The uncertainty, the simple possibility of a reward would drive mice to repeat a behavior unto their death. I began to understand why I had tried, and tried again, and tried again to heal my mother a little more with each class, each book, each experiment.

Through everything, I continued to go to therapy. And I learned to embrace my sleeplessness, working the night shift at the local gas station down the hill. I stayed away from alcohol. I dug into my classes. And I continued to thaw. Love entered my life in the form of an art history major who made me think and laugh, who made me dizzy with passion and cared for me with such gentleness that new ways of being began to open for me.

All of my fighting, all of my fleeing, all of my freezing and unthawing, my tending and befriending made a new way for me. Thanksgiving now meant a motley crew of sober siblings, children and grandparents, Harleys and tattoos.

That first holiday, I cut the turkey in the tiny apartment kitchen with the crowd looking on and sliced clear through my own hand. I'd never used a sharp knife like that before. Looking at the scar on my hand now, I say thank you, remembering the sense of belonging and care I cultivated, the community that held on to me as I fought and fled and unfroze sometimes so ungracefully. Together we tended the circle that always had room for one more—the circle that would heal us, drawing us out of a past it sometimes hurt to remember, into a future we never imagined.

Chapter 6

Take It In

A Little Bit of Love

In her book *Afterlife*, Julia Alvarez tells the story of a woman who has lost her husband to a sudden, massive heart attack. As she begins to reconstruct her life without her husband's physical presence in it, he starts showing up in ways that only she can sense, guiding her in her decisions, arguing with her in the car, loving her from beyond the grave. Soon, the woman's dead mother shows up in the same way, too. The mother offers advice about how to care for others in seemingly hopeless situations. The main character knows those situations are statistically improbable to improve no matter what she does. But her mother's voice winds its way through: "When nothing else can work," the woman remembers her saying, "let's see what love can do."

Love can work its way into improbable and impossible situations. Like water over a stone, it has the potential to wear down our suffering, create new pathways of possibility, and support life in inhospitable terrain. Love can't fix every situation, but it does have a way of working on us and opening portals to our closed hearts. Love keeps us company, settling in beside the unlikely good or the unlikely bad that comes our way. The house struck by lightning and set afire in the middle of the night. The child lost. The immigration case that goes well, or poorly. The lottery ticket and the car accident. The diagnosis and the deliverance from evil. None of it deserved, all of it happening all the same.

As much as I like to know the numbers, to spout off the statistics and the likelihood of this or that—knowing what to expect, be it good or bad—and as much as I like to be prepared, I'm writing about love because it so often is the culprit that comes in and steers things off course. Maybe it's the feeling that let you know they were the one, or the outstretched hand that held you back from falling off into the abyss. Maybe it was love that kept you alive or keeps you getting up in the morning. Maybe it is love for your companions on this earth that drives you with purpose to transform the world toward a justice you will never see.

Maybe when all else has failed, it can't hurt to see what love can do.

When you look at the sterile statistics, healing can seem unlikely for many of us. For instance, the long-term recovery rate for alcoholism hovers between 22 and 33 percent, depending on what studies you read. Adverse childhood experiences, or ACEs—like witnessing violence in the home, experiencing violence, abuse, or neglect, or having a parent in prison or living with active addiction or mental illness—tend to result in adverse adult experiences— like increased rates of mental illness, chronic health problems, and substance abuse in the surviving child. Systemic racism, poverty, and other forms of oppression can compound the negative effects of these adverse childhood experiences, making help hard or impossible to find. Going on statistics alone, it would be fair to say that many of us were never meant to survive.

But we are more than statistics, more than numbers and diminished possibilities. And love's best work comes into play when things seem dire, reminding us that we are full human beings with a past and a present and maybe even a future. The love we give and receive can change us. The stories we tell about our survival can chart a new way for us and for others.

When I went to my first recovery meeting, I was thirteen. I was a responsible kid on the whole—super responsible, to be exact. I ran my own baking business, volunteered at church, made family dinners most nights, and did my best to keep my family from going too far off the rails. Nobody knew I was drinking and getting high every day, too.

I didn't drink like the other kids my age; that had been clear for some time. One middle school sleepover with my childhood girlfriends proved that fact beyond the shadow of a doubt. The older brother had brought down a bottle of whiskey, and the two of us went drink for drink while my friends looked on in horror. It was the last time I hunkered down in my Holly Hobbie sleeping bag with those friends. It hurt to be looked at the way they saw me now—and truth be told, they probably weren't all that interested in hanging around with me after I kissed their older brother, either.

So I started hanging out with the neighborhood kids instead, running with the girls who were sixteen and seventeen and eighteen years old—the ones who were dropping out of school to get their GEDs. Letting them guide me with my hair and makeup and boyfriends, beginning to live the double life that would become all too familiar: straight As at school in the gifted program by day, terrors by night that no one would believe, anyway.

My first trip to a recovery meeting had a relatively mild beginning. I had been caught getting high at a babysitting job, and the mom of the family insisted that we sit down with my father to talk about it. This mom cared about me, and she paid attention. Sure, she was the mother of my boyfriend, who was serving time at the juvenile detention center. And sure, she got high with her teenage kids on the regular when they were home on passes, but for whatever reason she looked at me differently. She paid attention to what I was up to, taking me out for ice cream after our Saturday visits to see her son. Even though she had long ago given up on the possibility that her kids might succeed in some sort of traditional way, she held out hope for me.

The night I was babysitting, I waited until I had put the baby in my care to bed and they were sound asleep before I snuck down into the basement to light up. I smoked just a little. Enough to create the smell, but not enough to make me high. And I waited for that mom to come home. Sure enough, she busted me, and the next day we sat together with my father in her living room as the dam burst. I came out with the truth about my drinking and drug use. My father sat there in shock, not quite believing what I said was true. All the same, I was grounded—and recovery meetings, school, and church were my only outs. So off I went.

At thirteen, it was hard to see how a program that suggested not drinking could apply to me. Hard to imagine myself as anything like the old men seated around the table, hard to comprehend how I could or would work this program of recovery when I had zero interest in giving up drinking and drugs. They were tools critical to my survival. I soon learned I could walk in one door of a meeting while my father watched and walk right out the back door and get high, coming back through an hour later on the dot for my ride home.

Sometimes I'd show up at a meeting or two by choice, searching for a shot at a life I could live. But the double life of external success and internal suffering was taking its toll. So by the time I made my way back to recovery at the age of twenty-two, I was ready. I knew the drill: Go to a meeting every day. Don't drink. Read the recovery literature. Talk to people. Get a sponsor and work the steps.

I also knew I couldn't and wouldn't do most of these things, so I turned my attention to the first two. I stopped drinking, and I went to a meeting every day. Already, I knew to take what I needed and leave the rest.

I knew enough to join a meeting where I wouldn't know anyone. Somewhere I could let my guard down as best I could. The Polish Catholic church in town had a 7:00 a.m. group that met every morning. I didn't know it then, but I learned later that there is something about morning for me, something about showing up before I have a chance to armor up for the day that made all the difference.

There in the basement of the church, more than fifty people would show up each morning and seat themselves in concentric circles, drinking bad coffee and watching the ants crawl by on the ancient carpet. Around us were pictures of a very white, very blond, long-haired, Gregg Allman–style Jesus on the walls and cross-stitch sayings like "One Day at a Time" and "First Things First."

Each morning that I showed up and sat down without running from the room counted as a win. It took me about a week to notice that wherever I sat in that meeting, two older women would sit right behind me. One of them looked like my grandmother, her long white hair wrapped tightly on the top of her head in a bun. The two of them were in their seventies, and they were kind and funny. Each morning they'd find me and set themselves down, gently and consistently asking me how I was and making a few suggestions. Why don't you sit up front, they'd say, so that when the time to talk moves around the circle, you can join in? How many days have you gone without a drink now, they'd ask? Why don't you pick up a coin this morning?

I'd hate their suggestions, but they were always there, and they'd disarm me with their kindness. They'd show me pictures of their cats or draw me into a conversation about what they had been watching on TV the night before, which was always WWF—the World Wrestling Federation. When I told them how much trouble I was having sleeping and how hot it was in my un-air-conditioned apartment, they pooled their money and brought me a fan at the next meeting. When they suggested I start doing some reading about recovery and I said I couldn't afford the books, the books showed up on my seat the next day. When they asked me if I had gotten a sponsor yet—someone who could meet with me one on one and help me understand the program and help me work through the steps—I gathered up my courage over the course of a few weeks and chased the other dyke in the room out the door to ask for help.

That morning meeting full of old men and gentle women and bad coffee took me in, becoming a circle of love that started me healing, started me hoping for something just a little bit better. They weren't what I expected to find, but there they were: inviting me to join them for coffee, their motorcycles lined up one after another like shiny dominos, holding space on Main Street until the noon meeting in the next basement at the next church began. I didn't know it until they let me in, that these sober people were everywhere—these fiercely loyal, ferociously kind, sort of scary-looking people were there ready to lend a hand or take me in whenever I needed them, day or night.

Three years and a whole lot of sober days later, I moved away from that college town, starting seminary in another state. The morning I left, I drove the U-Haul truck to the meeting. I wanted one last dose of the love that would not let me go before I hit the road. Out there in the parking lot, the vet who had survived two tours as a Marine in Vietnam slipped a note into my hand. Put this in your wallet, he said, and don't lose it. I read it later: *Never be ashamed to lean on God*, he wrote. *People of faith have courage and you can, too. We're with you. Love, Kenny.*

The old ladies took down my address, later sending me notes of encouragement sealed up with stamps I knew took a tiny bit of their fixed income every month. For the next ten years, like clockwork, I'd get a call or a note from them on the anniversary of my sobriety. They circled me in their love all the way until they moved out into the great beyond.

Among the books I would soon be reading at seminary was the theologian Howard Thurman's writing about this kind of healing, unconditional, potential-filled love. An African American scholar and preacher born in 1899, Thurman was in many ways the spiritual backbone of the civil rights movement, offering up spiritual teachings written specifically for those living with their backs against the wall. The three books that Martin Luther King Jr. carried on his person were the Bible, the Constitution, and Howard Thurman's *Jesus and the Disinherited*. Thurman often said that a person had to first feel at home somewhere before they could feel at home anywhere. The folks at that 7:00 a.m. meeting gave me a place to call home, and from there, I could venture out surrounded by their love to make a home anywhere.

As a Christian, Thurman's understanding of this kind of healing love centers around Jesus, and the image he uses has Jesus holding a crown of goodness and righteousness above the heads of his people, urging them to grow tall enough to wear that crown. For him, this image is the embodiment of Jesus's unconditional love and power, meeting someone where they are and treating them as if they are already where they wish to be. This is the area where love operates, Thurman says. It is the kind of love that Jesus offered those he encountered, a holy, challenging, embracing love that can explode the limits of a situation and lift us into something more.

Now, I'm pretty sure this activist for Black liberation was not envisioning the long-haired white hippie Jesus of the paintings in the basement of that Polish Catholic church when he talked about Jesus holding a crown for us to grow tall enough to wear. And still, those people were there, the hands of god holding the crown taking shape in the gentle old ladies who carried pictures of their cats in their pockets. Present in the men who arrived early to make gallons of terrible coffee. There in the bikers with soft hearts who looked out for each other and me through those early days. All of us, holding up the crown of possibility, believing each other into the fulfillment of our possibilities, offering each other unconditional, healing love.

Not everyone who came into those basement doors stayed sober. We lost a lot of us. Love was not enough to heal us all. Life happened. Relapse happened. New folks arrived to either stay or go. The people in the circle shift and change, but the circle stays the same whatever city I land in—animated by a fierce, gentle, protective love—held by hands of every gender and color and history—all of us holding up a crown of hope and possibility for ourselves and each other.

Love cannot fix everything, but it can keep us company. It can help us imagine ourselves through the perspective of others, the ones who won't give up, who whisper through the ages, *Let's see what a little love can do.*

Part II

The hat

I want to find my hat,
the one I got in Provincetown.
That trip when we surprised ourselves
bought our wedding rings and
packed them away
hidden
in the sock drawer for years,
waiting.

I want to find my hat,
the one I grabbed every morning after our son was
born,
trying to hide my wild hair from the barista
on our early-morning walks
after too-short nights.

I want to find my hat,
the one I wore out running on my fortieth birthday,
when I proved that I could make it all the way
around the lake,
my improbable heart-close friend at my side.

TAKE WHAT YOU NEED

I want to find my hat,
quick comfort,
old self.

Swept up in the piles of soot and smoke and stink,
into the dumpster it went
without ceremony,
without
pause
on the day when it had to be done.

It was just a tan baseball hat
with a blue bill
fading from the sun,
frayed around the edges.

The daily companion.
The reminder of that trip we took together.

You getting up early
to fill the house
with smells of cinnamon and pastry
like you always did
friends laughing over coffee
in a rented condo
when everything was simple.

No children to carry from that burning house
no hearts to protect but our own

THE HAT

tender hopeful
battered bruised
still-healing hearts
daring to reach out
toward one another.

The equal sign emblazoned on the cap
clear message, simple code
I carried around
a way to recognize each other
queers and allies
that symbol
reminding me who I am
and who you are.
Equal. Worthy. Whole.
No matter what.

I don't want another hat,
thanks for asking.
I want that hat.
The history it held,
the sweat of the band,
the way we laughed at my terrible memory
standing in the Human Rights Campaign store in
Provincetown
so many years ago now,
wedding rings for someday
tucked secretly in our pockets.

Chapter 7

Take It Away

After the fire or the divorce or the diagnosis or the death, after leaving for college or taking off for a new start, after saying fuck you or flying off the handle, once we've told the truth about who we are, after we put down the drink or the drug or the cookie or the crack, there is always the next day.

Sure, the first night is dramatic as we walk out of our literal or metaphorical burning buildings with our beloveds, a bra, and a few photos in our hands—but bright as that moment is, and as important and painful as those moments are, they are only the beginning of the rest of our lives. Catching our breath, we realize that we are now the person whose house burned down, whose silence has ended, whose parent is dead. One moment it was one way, and now it is another. A piece of our identity has been added or lopped off, and it takes a whole lot longer than one day to learn how to live with it.

The night our house burned down, friends came to pick us up. Standing there in my Mickey Mouse T-shirt and gym shorts, dripping on their carpet, I realized that I was soaking wet. While the neighbors had taken the kids inside, I had kept vigil, watching the firefighters work. It was raining, a summer storm with lightning and thunder so powerful it woke up most of South Minneapolis, and I stood outside in it for hours. I was soaked. Physically numb, I had focused on one thing—survival for my family—a safe place to sleep, gathering up the few things we could carry when the fire was out. Shock, that survival tactic, had numbed me out and softened the initial blow.

Sometimes, we have to go back to those hard moments, those bright lines when things were one way once and are another way now, those times of a before and during and after that shape who we are. As much as I'd like to drive off into the sunset in my cherry-red muscle car screaming fuck you into the wind and let that be the end of the story, so often, it is only the beginning.

There's the first trip home after you've left for your new life, the walk through the house after your parent has died. There's living with the diagnosis you're only just beginning to accept as real, and there's always the not-so-glamorous third week at the new job you thought would change everything. There's year one and two and twenty of sober living. And chances are, before it gets all beautiful it is going to hurt.

Weeks after our house fire, the house remained gutted, the yard a mess. Slowdowns with our insurance company meant we couldn't clear the wreckage, and even after dozens of visits back to the house to salvage what we could, there was still so much more to do. It took a while for the go-ahead to empty the place, but eventually we gathered our resources and declared it Dumpster Day. We sifted through the debris one last time, without the benefit of shock's softening effect.

We planned to start at noon. We'd recruited help, and the people who loved us arrived in swarms, eager to do something to ease our pain and get this awful job done. When I walked up to the house, things were already underway. Not what I wanted. I had wanted to pray. To orient people to the tenderness of the task at hand. To remind them that this was our life, our children's lives, not just debris to be removed. I wanted the day to feel sacred. I wanted to say thank you. Instead, I was met with a team already high energy and underway. After weeks of having so much out of our control, here was one more loss, even as people acted with love.

Boxes of twenty-gallon garbage bags lined the entry when I walked in. Industrial brooms, masks, and gloves flanked the door for folks to take. Everything left in the house had been declared too damaged to keep, and all of it had to go. More than 2,600 items went out the door and into the dumpster that day. I know because in the weeks ahead I completed the inventory required by the insurance company. A long list naming each item, the approximate date when we purchased it, and how much it would cost to replace. Even with a whole lot of help, completing that inventory hurt like hell, each item on the list forcing me to call up the memory of its origin story— story after story from a life that no longer felt like ours.

After years of accumulating no more than I could carry in my car, I had finally settled down in my thirties. My wife and I had more than matching luggage. We had matching furniture in a house that we loved. Our kids didn't know what it was to live out of a backpack aside from our summer adventures on the road, and I had never wanted them to find out. Never wanted to return to that life myself after fighting so hard to leave it behind.

We'd been through the doors into this house a million times before that day—searching for stuffed animals and baby blankets, looking for the bins of special things we'd saved for the kids, scrapbooks, photographs, Christmas decorations and favorite toys, journals, jewelry, family dishes and silverware. We looked for it all—but we never could have looked enough.

So much went out those doors. Those oh-so-kind people who didn't know the stories, didn't touch the things tenderly, they had to get the job done. They were ripping up the mattress we slept on, the king-size bed we'd finally been able to afford that fit us all—they were digging into it with a knife, chopping it into pieces because it was too heavy, too wet and moldy to toss down the stairs.

A few of our friends noticed our shaky hearts and took us in different directions, trying, I think, to protect us from watching it all unfold. My wife went into the basement to sort through holiday decorations and pack away photos. I headed upstairs with my recovery crew to the epicenter of the fire, sorting through what remained of our bedroom and my books. One young woman stayed by my side that day. Returning to the rooms of recovery after the death of her boyfriend, she knew loss and grief, sudden and raw like mine. She led me to a spot on the floor and brought me book after book, each one a metaphorical brick in the fortress I had built to bring me into this new life. Together we went through them all. I touched the wet pages like the sacrament that they were, leafing through the dog-eared places, praying I could memorize them as they passed one last time through my hands.

You know how holding something in your hands sometimes helps you remember?

The memories came flooding back as I sat up there on the floor. *Get a Financial Life*—the book the college gave us when we graduated. Strunk and White's *The Elements of Style*—a parting gift from my high school English teacher. Poems and stories, the twenty-five hearts, each one inscribed with a love note, tucked into the copy of *Alice in Wonderland* my first girlfriend gave me twenty-five years ago for Christmas, each one fluttering out as I flipped through the pages. Each book brought a memory flashing by and flooding in and I tried to grab them, to hold them all, afraid that with the physical item gone the memories would be lost forever.

When someone we love is dying, sometimes the biggest thing we fear is forgetting them. Forgetting their face, their smell, their voice, the touch of their hands.

When my mother was dying, I tried to memorize her voice. When my well-meaning stepsister changed the outgoing message on the answering machine just days after her death, I fell apart.

With all of the activity happening on Dumpster Day, I didn't realize until it was too late that no one was keeping watch, holding vigil over all that went out the door that day. Neighbors and strangers and friends had emptied our house before we knew it. The metaphorical message on the answering machine had been erased, and all of it was gone.

Two twenty-foot dumpsters sat on the curb, filled to the brim with our stuff, with the pickers arriving to sort through these treasure-trove boxes faster than we could tie the tarps on. Please, I begged them. Please wait until I am gone. I can't watch you rummage through the remnants of our life, I can't watch you walk away with our children's toys. Please, just wait until I am gone. Then you can take what you need and leave the rest behind.

At the end of that terrible day, our hearts were understandably broken. When we went back to our temporary home that night, my wife and I were wrecked. Back in our bedroom, the kids tucked in and sleeping, the second round of pain set in. Our minds started to race. "Did you find this?" she asked. "How about that?" I wondered. "How could we have forgotten to look for that?" we panicked. "We should have gone through their rooms again," we said. "Did anyone salvage the Disney pins? What about the top drawer from my dresser?" my wife asked. "The letters, the pictures, the ring from my aunt? Why didn't we go through that?"

I knew the answer to that question. Her dresser had been obliterated in the fire. The bedroom was the epicenter of it all, lightning striking just a few feet above our heads as we slept, and there wasn't much left to it. I'd sorted through the wet rubble of insulation, our roof open to the sky. There was nothing left in that room to save.

I said all of this, and it was not enough. I reminded us how much time we'd spent in that now-toxic house—sorting and searching for the things we could remember to find. There was no way we could have gotten it all, no way to remember everything that mattered, no way to save so much of it even if we wanted to. But logic wasn't cutting it, and we were swirling quickly down the rabbit hole of despair when something in me sat up.

"We can't do this," I said. "We have to stop. We can't blame ourselves for the things we've lost, the things we didn't remember to look for. We can't make this any worse. It already hurts so much I can hardly bear it. If we turn on ourselves and each other, we aren't going to make it."

I didn't know to name this as self-compassion at the time. Didn't know there were whole books written on it as the new old way to inner peace. I only knew that if we got into a blame game with ourselves or started pointing fingers at each other we would crumble. We couldn't afford to add self-inflicted wounds to this pile of pain. Something inside of me wanted to survive that fire and all that it meant, even when it hurt.

Determined not to sabotage myself by taking an already bad situation and making it worse, I went back through the events of the day. I took the advice from those sleepless nights in early sobriety, when a friend taught me that instead of lying there in the dark watching myself go from zero to *I suck* in sixty seconds, I could make a list of things I was grateful for instead.

Make it a game, they suggested. Start with A and go all the way to Z, listing something you are grateful for with every letter of the alphabet. I didn't alphabetize at the end of Dumpster Day, but I did decide to stop beating myself up with regret, turning my attention to something else.

Instead of remembering the things I had lost, I listed the people who had shown up.

There was the dear one who organized a crew of people from my Saturday-morning recovery meeting, all of them pulling gloves and boots from their cars and marching into our stinking, molding house.

There was the newly sober one who sat by my side as we went through my library, seeing and saying goodbye to the treasures from high school and college and graduate school.

There was the kind woman from church who stumbled across my green three-ring binder from my time in psychotherapy in Chicago, the one that listed out my treatment plan and held a hundred deeply personal journal entries. She handed it to me gently when she dug it out of the debris, saying simply, "I think you will probably want this"—instead of pitching it away.

There was the friend who took on the thankless task of leading us through the day, thinking of everything from gloves to brooms to dumpsters and tarps.

Listing the people who showed up to help could keep me busy forever. I didn't need to list my failures and hurts.

I asked myself then—and many times after—instead of turning on ourselves or others for mistakes real and perceived that we have made, what if we remembered the love that ensured we never went without even when we lost everything? What if I looked at the story that way?

On that night full of fresh grief, the sparkling web of connection we had created was holding us close, each person a dewdrop jewel. Living into this loss, this new identity, would take time. If we could let the story hold it all, remembering the love sitting right next to the loss, we just might make it—and have everything we need.

Chapter 8

Take Another Little Piece of My Heart

Growing up, I didn't know much about grief. My mother cried often and expressed her emotions freely, but none of it felt safe or grounded in reality. My father teared up twice over the course of my childhood—once when it was time for the cat to go to the vet and never return, and once when my grandmother died. Crying was acceptable at the funeral home, in private, but otherwise feelings should be tucked in close, tamped down. Feelings were dangerous, and grief was a luxury for other people better equipped to handle it.

When I was pregnant with our daughter, I read everything I could get my hands on about childbirth. While this was our second child, it was the first child I was carrying and the first and only time I would be pregnant. Plus, several years earlier when we were having our son, my wife declared early on that she would be having a C-section. No labor for her. I had no idea what to expect—so I turned to my old friends, books, to chart the course.

I latched on to the writings of Ina May Gaskin. Gaskin lives on a commune in Iowa called the Farm and is the author of *Spiritual Midwifery*, a text that shifted the story of what pregnancy and labor and birth could look like. Some of my friends dismissed this obsessive study of mine as a return to my Grateful Dead–following hippie days, but I am forever grateful for what I learned.

Gaskin talks about birth as a natural process. Something your body knows how to do, like breathing. The most important part of participating in the birth of your child is to surrender to the wisdom of your body. To listen for the signs and signals of what you need and follow them, whether they make sense in the moment or not. If you want to move, move, she says. If you are hungry, eat, even though the people at the hospital will freak out if you do. If something in you says to switch to a different position, do it. Let go of your schedule and your self-consciousness. Trust yourself, your body, and the team you've assembled around you. And then settle in for the ride.

I think about Ina May Gaskin every time I accompany someone who is grieving. The world can feel so out of control when loss comes, and we can wonder if we will ever function fully again. The exhaustion, the anger, the tears—they can all feel like too much, and people around us often try to be helpful but aren't. They tell us about the five stages of grief, as if anyone ever progressed through loss on a schedule. They tell us to count our blessings when all we can see is our pain. They expect us to come back to work after three days of bereavement leave or none at all.

I keep learning that when pain runs deep, you have to stop caring about your clothes, or what time you are supposed to be somewhere next, or who is watching. You simply have to surrender. Trusting that our bodies and hearts and minds were made to face loss with grief. Every one of our ancestors lost someone they loved, and we will, too. And just like we know how to give birth and make love and breathe without understanding everything about the technical exchange of oxygen, we know how to grieve and die, and we know how to mourn. We just have to surrender to it, and some of us are better at that than others.

Surrendering isn't my strong suit. I've earned my buttoned-up British ancestry, my mastery of composure.

My first lesson in grief came when I was twelve. As I was sitting in my middle school math class, the call came in from the front office. My parents were waiting for me. I needed to gather my things and go. I knew this could only mean one thing: that my grandmother had died. It was the only possible outcome of her cancer, of the color yellow that had seeped into her eyes and the beds of her fingernails.

I remember holding in my tears during my last visit with her at the hospital, on the long walk down the hallway at school, and through the car ride to the funeral home where we picked out a casket. I saw my father cry for the first time that day, and I cried silently, too, clenching my jaw. *I will not lose control*, I told myself. This loss would bring chaos beyond what I could imagine. I knew there was no room for my keening even as the questions bubbled up inside.

Who would kneel with me now beside the bed at night, lifting up prayers from our hearts that passed out through our pressed fingertips, up to the ears of god? I could not find the ears of god now. My grandmother was gone, and she took the comfort of those prayers with her. She took the part of me that trusted this world, that lap on the La-Z-Boy recliner in the den, soap operas on the TV and butter mints passed out like the joy they were, my head snuggled into her soft chest. At twelve years old, I knew that surrendering to the sadness was not an option. The loss was too deep, the pain too much to bear without her.

It took thirty years and a whole lot of therapy to begin to learn how to ride the waves of love and loss, to remember that my body and spirit knew how to do this thing that felt so scary. Not surprisingly, it was my kids who showed me the way.

It was a few weeks after the fire, and we'd all begun to settle in to the rental house that would be our home for the next ten months. Four hand-carved parrots kept watch on the posts of my daughter's twin bed as I read her a bedtime story. When the story ended, her five-year-old questions began. "Did we lose this in the fire?" she wanted to know. "How about that?" She peppered me with questions, taking most of my answers in stride. But then we got to the one that would ultimately undo her. "What about Buckle Bear?" she asked. Surely Buckle Bear had survived.

Buckle Bear was a large stuffed animal covered in different multicolored, multipatterned straps that crossed its chest, each one with a different kind of closure. We had gotten it for our daughter when she was just eighteen months old to keep her occupied as we drove across the country, making our move from New York to Minnesota. She loved that bear, spending hours buckling and unbuckling, snapping and unsnapping all of its different closures on that trip and in the years since. I knew the bear was a goner the day I'd walked through her room, and as soon as I left the house, I started a search for a replacement, but I came up empty-handed.

As a parent, I promised myself that no matter what, I wouldn't lie to the kids. This was an absolute for me. I wanted them to know that they could trust me even and especially when we were hurting. So I said it: "Buckle Bear is gone, honey. We lost him in the fire."

Her small body shifted. Silence, then a sound erupted from her tiny frame that I had never heard before and hope never to hear again. A moan, a wail, a deep, guttural *No*. Her sounds brought everyone else in the house running. First to arrive was her brother, with my wife right on his heels. "What happened?" they asked, sure she was hurt. "It's Buckle Bear," I said. "I told her when she asked, that he's gone."

At eight years old, her big brother knew exactly what to do. He crawled right into that creepy twin-sized bed and held her. "I know," he kept saying. "I know." A moment later my wife climbed into the bed, too, holding him as he held her. Soon everyone was crying.

Somehow I was both in the moment and observing it. Always the practical one, I worried that this tiny, hand-carved antique bed might collapse under our collective weight, becoming the first security deposit casualty of our time at the house if I climbed in, too, so I stayed kneeling on the floor next to them, wrapping my arms around this weeping pile of my beloveds. They were wailing, sobbing, holding on to each other in their loss.

We stayed there for a long time. Crying. Telling stories about Buckle Bear. We remembered together how we'd chosen Buckle Bear for Kate because at six months old she'd unhooked the straps on her car seat, and ever since then we'd called her our little Houdini. We'd hoped that by giving her Buckle Bear, he'd distract her from unbuckling her car seat on the long ride across the country. And he did. The buckles were harder; the snaps made a satisfying sound when she closed them and popped open when she squeezed the edges just right.

As we told the stories, Kate's older brother, Henry, piped in. "You know," he said, "I never understood why you called it Buckle Bear. It was a monkey, not a bear."

"No way," the rest of us said. "It was definitely a bear."

"Oh yeah? Then why did it have a tail?"

That stumped us. The next day I got online and looked again, and sure enough, there it was: the Buckle Monkey. I placed our order. One strappy, multicolored, multipatterned glorious Buckle Monkey/Bear traveled across the country after a night of grief and loss, stories and connection.

My family taught me something about grief that night, about letting the loss roll through you like a wave, unstopped by bedtimes or rickety four-poster beds or even decades of disbelief that grief could be held and released in a way that would not kill me. I learned that we would survive the pain, that I could survive the crying and the tears. That the loss would not in fact crack me into a million pieces and send me swirling off into a great abyss. We would cry, and we would comfort each other, and we would laugh with the tears still wet on our faces. And we would not let each other go.

I still don't like to cry. I don't like to let down my guard and feel that vulnerable or that sad. I'd rather make something or break something or walk until my feet hurt. Out there on my own, I always worried that if I allowed the crying to start, it would never stop. But lately, I've been trying to let it flow. I've been calling on my ancestors for strength. Stomping around the lake near my house, I ask my grandmother to come in close. I draw on my friends, past and present, here and gone, and ask them to walk with me. I remember the love that has held me, kept me tethered to this world, and touched me with the spark of life that lives in me. I remember that alone or with others, there is a love that will not let me go, and in my own way I let myself cry, tears falling silently down my face.

Chapter 9

Give and Take

Never own more than you can fit in your car. I lived by that simple policy for the first twenty-five years of my life. As a teenager and young adult, I moved often, packing up every six months or so to go from this dorm room to that apartment, then later from this city to that one. The mantra helped me leave on a moment's notice without being weighed down by things. At the time, I told myself it was part of my rebel mindset, that I was a minimalist. Smug and superior, I didn't need things to define me. Nothing could hold me down. I was free to grab this opportunity or go on that adventure.

It was only when I was in my early forties that I realized that was only one part of the story. Closing up the office at church one night, I met with the youth coordinator coming careening in. Balancing an overstuffed backpack on one arm and a pile of books in the other, she barely made it to the couch before she collapsed. When I commented on how much she was carrying, she replied, "Yeah, I guess since my parents' divorce, I just feel more comfortable carrying everything I need around with me wherever I go." Her words reminded me of my own choice and the decisions we make for safety, security, or a way out.

We moved around a lot, as I mentioned. On the surface, it looked like I was rooted. My family lived in the same house from the time I was one until my mom died when I was thirty-six. But when I was a kid, my mom got sick a lot. Often happening suddenly, her illness would have my brother and me shipped out on a moment's notice to stay with a neighbor or a friend or a family member for unknown periods of time. Sometimes we'd get to pack a bag, sometimes we wouldn't. Sometimes whatever we happened to have on us would have to be enough. At a young age, I got to know I didn't need much. My stuffed hippo, a book, and some clean underwear could keep me going for a long time.

When I got a little older, I started running away on a regular basis. And my backpack became the holder of all the things I really needed. I added clean socks and Little Debbie snack cakes, a bottle for water, and Chunky bars to my pack. Along with my school supplies, I figured I had everything I needed. I also began planning ahead, strategically amassing a stockpile by the shelter I'd built in the woods across the river. It included things that might be suspicious if I snuck them out all at once: several cans of Chef Boyardee ravioli (buried to avoid detection), a pocketknife with can opener, fishing gear, and a bucket (to put out my fire in case of emergency). I wanted to be ready to go on a moment's notice. I wanted to make sure I had what I needed if I was forced to leave the rest behind.

When the house fire hit, I was forty-two—living very differently for some time. I'd gotten married, acquired some really nice furniture, gone to graduate school, built a literal library of books, had two kids who liked their things, and taken on a serious job that required me to put down roots and stay awhile in a community. I learned the joy of cozy things: matching towels, soft sheets, and a down comforter of my own. I allowed myself to loosen up on my rules—and it wasn't just rules about the things we needed and how many items could fit in a backpack, or even the car. I had loosened the rules about going it alone. I learned to let people in, no longer under the illusion I could take care of everything myself. This new way of living didn't come from a virtuous acceptance of the spiritual reality that I preached as a pastor, of Martin Luther King Jr.'s "Inescapable network of mutuality, tied in a single garment of destiny." No, my learning to lean into the love that others had to give came out of necessity. It came through my second college roommate, the community of misfits I was gathered into, and the recovery ladies and others who taught me sobriety meant relying on a "we" more than an "I."

This wasn't an easy area of growth for me in college, and even with a family, a church, a community, it still feels more natural for me to push others away than to let them in. Most of the time, I'd rather struggle with something on my own even when it's obvious to everyone around me that a little assistance would ease the way. I'd always rather be helping others than having them help me. Trusting that people will show up in the ways that they say they will doesn't come naturally. And I've been actively working on these challenges for over twenty years. I may still not be the best at asking for and accepting help, but I've made progress.

What I've gotten good at is bringing people into my life who know me. And I've learned to keep them close.

The day after our house fire, I showed up at the church office to hand off my responsibilities. Given the fact that I didn't yet have a pair of clean underwear, let alone a dress shirt, it didn't seem like I'd be able to do much for a little while. Once we handled all the practicalities like preaching dates and payroll, I made my way to the classroom where my kids were playing with the director of children, youth, and family ministries. She came over to me. "I've done some research," she said, "and one of the recommendations for kids who've suffered a loss like this is to ask them for a list of comfort items—things that make them feel at home wherever they are—and start replacing them as soon as possible. Can you help them make a list and let me know what's on it? And oh yeah," she said, "can you make one for yourselves, too?"

Grateful for her thoughtfulness, I agreed. It was easy to make the lists with the kids, easy to let people help them. I discovered it was so much harder when it came to myself.

We joked that day that my new spiritual practice was going to be saying yes when people offered to help. "You can be choosy about who you let in," she said, and turn away things that aren't actually helpful. "But," she added, "you might want to consider saying yes a whole lot more than you're inclined to."

I couldn't imagine anything more awful. And yet the depth of our need was so great, I couldn't say no. Turns out she wasn't joking. Soon I would be saying yes with all the dedication of a regular spiritual practice—with intention, with regularity, and in hopes of connecting with something larger than myself. My story was about to shift from saying I suck at asking for help to yes and thank you and holy shit this is hard.

My first major opportunity with this spiritual practice came in the form of pants.

I know I probably shouldn't tell you this, but the truth is that for the first dozen or more years of my ministry I wore the same pair of black suit pants to church every Sunday. They were the pants I'd worn to see the Ministerial Fellowship Committee—the body that gives you a thumbs-up or thumbs-down for ordination—and I considered them my lucky pants. I didn't do Sundays without them.

I am not a fan of clothes shopping, as you can probably guess from the fact that I had one pair of Sunday pants that I wore for twelve years. Going into the clothing section of any store makes my skin crawl. I've never fit the mold of femininity (or masculinity), and while I think that I clearly read as a woman, that hasn't been my experience in real life. I

get "sirred" regularly, especially when we are traveling or when someone hears my deeper-than-average
voice without looking up to see my face. Most kids
think I'm a dude. Folks don't see me the way I see
myself. This summer, when my niece was visiting,
she confessed that when she was little, she didn't get
it that her aunt Loretta and I were gay because she
always thought I was a man.

I hear all this—I've heard it for years—and I still
don't get it. I have fairly enormous breasts. They're
verifiably huge. That's part of why Loretta told me
to grab a bra from our still smoldering house the
night of the fire. I literally cannot walk into a store
and buy a bra anywhere. The whole process is an
ordeal of measuring and hoping and online ordering
and enormous contraptions with twenty-plus hooks
arriving in the mail from Sweden. Do people really
think these are man boobs?

I am tall and big. I have short hair, and if given
the choice I'll dress casually, wearing a T-shirt
and jeans, maybe a favorite hoodie in the winter. I
don't wear makeup, and when it comes time to go
to work, I intentionally dress myself from a prese-
lected assortment of outfits. I have my closet organized by work clothes and nonwork clothes, and all
of my shirts and jackets matched with my previously

mentioned lucky pants. I can't stand to have my emotional energy sucked up and my mojo destroyed by self-doubt when it comes time to get dressed and stand up in front of hundreds of people, giving them a glimpse into my soul while staying inspirational, truth-telling, and externally composed. I need to keep the outside polished, and I can't spend twenty minutes losing my shit in front of the closet in the morning. I have to keep things simple.

With our house fire, I lost most of my clothes. The carefully selected matching outfits for church, the worn-out flannel shirts tucked in the back of the closet, the tank top I wore to get my first tattoo, the lucky pants—all gone.

As a professional, I no longer slipped on my black leather jacket and biker boots whenever I left the house, but at least I had my lucky pants. My Sunday-morning armor. Until they were gone.

Soon after the fire, a member of the church called and invited our family over for dinner. Let us feed you, she said, plus you and I are the same size and you need some clothes to wear. She was right, of course, god bless her. We were the same size, and I did need some clothes. The gym shorts and Mickey Mouse shirt I left the house in weren't going to be enough for Sunday morning or even the next week. I said yes.

Unlike me, you could tell that she liked to shop and that she had instinctively good taste. She walked me through her closet and brought out beautiful thing after beautiful thing, noticing the way that certain styles made my body look and selecting the pieces that made me look and feel my best. It was an incredibly loving gesture, not just because she probably gave me more than $1,000 worth of clothing but because she thought of things I couldn't and didn't think of, things I needed to be thinking about but couldn't handle on my own quite yet.

It felt strange stepping up onto the chancel of the church wearing someone else's pants. My lucky pants were gone. The ten-plus-year-old talisman of luck and protection. But I was learning something new. I was learning to say yes, and thank you, as I let people in. I was learning to accept help that I desperately needed, even when I wanted nothing to do with it.

There was kindness in the way that woman helped me. How she fed my family and took me on a tour of her closet. How she sent me home with just what I needed.

Several weeks later on a Saturday night, I took a deep breath, said some prayers, and walked into Talbots an hour before closing. I set my sights on the kindest-looking salesperson I could find, and I asked her to outfit me, head to toe, with a new suit and anything else I needed. She put me in a dressing room and lined things up: pants and shirts and jackets in a couple of sizes, followed by accessories— matching scarves, necklaces, and earrings that intentionally went together and landed at the right spot on my chest with the new shirts she had picked out. I left with a silky blue blouse and a new black suit, matching earrings, and a necklace—all things I never would have picked out on my own. I paid at the register with a gift card a member of the church had given me, a note tucked inside acknowledging all of the loss I was facing and naming all of the love that was surrounding me.

Leaving the store, I felt so many things. Exhausted and sad, grateful to have accomplished this Herculean task that almost no one would understand as Herculean. I sat in the car and took it all in for a minute. The yuck of standing in that store, of wearing clothing not my own, of people saying all the wrong things. The gift of people helping me in exactly the ways I needed help. I paused to let it all in. My car was full of hangers and bags of clothing—beautiful, elegant, simple clothing given to me with love. It wouldn't replace my lucky pants, but it would surround me with love. I was learning to say yes.

Learning to let my heart and my car and sometimes even my eyes overflow. I was learning to let go of the stories that once served me well and start writing something new.

A friend of mine says that we come by most of our stories about ourselves honestly. Some nugget in the narrative is true, some piece of hard-earned wisdom in the story serves to help us. But sometimes, she says, those stories no longer serve us. Sometimes our stories turn misguided, like a missile, and threaten harm in the new terrain of our ever-evolving lives.

I still like to pack up my car with my kids and my wife and the dogs and drive off into the sunset. I still like to be free. To trust that I have what I need. When I can manage to say yes to the support all around me, security is no longer about the few things I can fit into the car. It's about letting in the love that surrounds me.

I can still be choosy: About who I let in. About what I say no to, when it doesn't help. And I can still say yes with intention, with regularity, and with the hope of connecting to something larger than myself. And when those yeses happen, I can feel myself a part of that inescapable network of mutuality, knit into that single garment of destiny that will not let me go.

Part III

Hold it all

Remember
even when it hurts so much it takes your breath away
remember the way you survived
the hard-won way through
remember the way it never got all the way to you
did not take you down
remember the way you pulled yourself
crawling gasping dragging out the other side
of that to this
Recovering, yes, for some time
Rebuilding, maybe, forever
But here
Still here

Holding hoping living
Remember the dear ones—
ancestors, strangers, friends—
who held your head, held your hand, held your heart
when you could hold nothing—
not even your own breathing steady
Remember the cleansing tears that would not stop, the
way you felt whole

TAKE WHAT YOU NEED

for a moment
when your body moved or the words came out the way
you intended
and you felt like yourself again
Remember when your brain worked fast your thoughts
coming clear and then dissolving—
but there they were, and there you were, returning,
broken and whole and new and old all at once,
cracked but holding,

Which way will you choose?
What will you lose?
It's something either way.
Lose the pain if you let your grip loosen all the way to
letting go,
inviting oblivion to carry you into the great beyond.
Lose the open wound the free pass well earned if you
push back against the pull down of grief
Lose the gold you can pull from this shit if you forget, if
you dare not to remember

What if there was no choice to make
no thing to lose—
What if you knew you could hold it all
That you were made for this
Repair, resilience, surrender and survival
Container of multitudes
Both and
instead of either

HOLD IT ALL

What if you held it all?
Everything that happened and all that is happening now
All of it
No right or wrong
No this or that
Beauty and longing, love and loss, pain and percep-
tion, joy,
Content.
Holding it lightly, no tight grip
All of it passing through like water
These grateful cupped hands.

Chapter 10

The Training Takes Hold

The night of the fire, I was simultaneously freakishly calm and completely out of my mind. Gathering us up to get out of the house I now knew was on fire, I kept saying to my son, "Get your shoes. Get your shoes and get your sister's shoes and meet me at the front door." He kept going off and coming back with one or two shoes, but not all of them, and I'd send him back on his mission. Somehow it felt like we had time for this.

When we finally all gathered at the front door, probably a total of forty-five seconds later, we walked out one by one. I turned back, remembering all of the emergency training I'd received at different jobs. Leave the door open and unlocked. You don't want the firefighters searching for a key or having to pause to break down the door. Leave it open.

Something in me knew that we were stepping over more than a simple threshold that night, that we needed to welcome the help that was on its way, or at least not block it. With each step, we were moving away from life as we'd known it into some new, unimaginable place. We had to welcome it, even if we didn't want it. Alarms blaring and rain falling, I unlocked the door, left it swinging open on its hinges, and we all walked out of that house.

I didn't know this moment was coming—couldn't have prepared for it if I'd tried, despite all the books I'd read later that told me how to properly inventory my house. Maybe this is how it is. We can worry and wonder and plan how we might respond to a wide variety of possible scenarios, but when they come, they're never quite what we expected. I never saw a global pandemic or a house fire—or this love that changed my life—coming. Never knew my heart could open this wide or break this much.

I do know that all of the emergency training I've had and all of the asking for help and community building I'd been doing before these moments changed my response, and I'm grateful for that. I know that our preparation matters. And I know that when the transformational moments come, we can't always be graceful. We won't always step over the threshold leaving the door unlocked, but I am learning to try.

Arundhati Roy encourages us to experience the portals presented to us with intention and choice. When we experience a transformational moment, a gateway that can take us from this place to that, she writes in "The Pandemic Is a Portal," "We can choose to walk through it, dragging the carcasses of our prejudice and hatred, our avarice, our data banks and dead ideas, our dead rivers and smoky skies behind us. Or we can walk through lightly, with little luggage, ready to imagine another world. And ready to fight for it."

Writing about our world at large and how traumatic moments can open a door that was previously locked, she notes the choices that help us change our relationships with ourselves, the environment, and each other. I think her writing rings true for us as individuals, too. There are transformational moments, thresholds and portals in our lives that we will move through whether we like it or not. God knows I did not want that fire. We can't control when they come or what they look like no matter how well we prepare, but we can control how we will approach them, what we will carry, and what we will leave behind. Maybe, in time, we will learn to do as she suggests and "walk through lightly, carrying little luggage, ready to imagine another world. And ready to fight for it." Maybe we'll even do it gracefully sometimes.

The thing is, I'm really good at coaching other people. I can tell you how to approach change with an open heart all day long. My job means I've gotten to accompany hundreds of folks through transformational moments, cheering them along their way. I can quote poetry and psychology, theology and spiritual traditions from around the globe. I have so many great suggestions for others that you probably want to kick me in the shins. And when it comes to my own life, I'm always a little bit disappointed to find that I'm just like everybody else, kicking and screaming along the way when the portal opens and beckons me inside.

In my role as a minister, I've often seen those portals once closed and locked swing open with possibility at the time of death—when the veil between one world and the next is noticeably thin—when old hurts loosen their grip, or roles reverse and the child is now in charge as the parent slips away. Whatever it is that happens at the sacred time of death, I've seen hearts swing open on their hinges.

I thought I knew all about this. And then my mom got sick. In June of 2011 I got the call that my mom had stage 4 lung cancer. She died in early August. By the time she was diagnosed, the cancer had spread from her lungs to her bones and her brain, and she was in significant pain. She had gone to the doctor because of problems with her legs, and a CT scan revealed the cancer. We knew it was bad as soon as we heard the news, but none of us realized quite how bad until chemo began. The doctor said the chemo had little chance of stopping the progression of the cancer, but it was the only thing that might keep the tumor in her spine from pressing on her spinal cord and paralyzing her. And you never know, sometimes you hit it out of the park, the doctor added. I hated him for that.

My mom held on to those two comments from the doctor with a literal death grip. She launched into intensive chemotherapy that made her sicker by the day. She wanted to live so badly—to have more time with her kids and grandkids—and she was scared. So very scared. Death was approaching like an oncoming train, and she was not ready.

At the time, I was part of a ministry team at a large church in western New York. I'd just had a baby—our second child—and the two senior ministers were away on sabbatical. I juggled everything as best I could, making the trip south to Maryland to be there for doctor's appointments and visits and then days and weeks to help with caring for my mom at home and in hospice. I juggled my nursing baby, my adjusting three-year-old, being present in my marriage, and supporting my wife through a job change. The church I served and the colleagues I shared the ministry with were amazing, offering the time and space that I needed and telling me things I did and did not want to hear.

"Losing a mother is a big deal," they kept saying. "This will be rough."

"You don't understand," I tried to convince them. "She is in so much pain, and she is so scared. Caring for her at home is getting harder and harder, and her quality of life is terrible. I'm trying to make this work, but this pull of wanting to be with her and wanting to be anywhere but with her—of trying to take care of my kids and my family and my church, all while I'm trying to take care of her—it's too much. We can't go on like this. It's too hard. Death will be a relief. There's no good way out of this situation."

To my closest ones, I'd acknowledge the deeper truth: that I'd lost my mother a long time ago. She lived with a mental illness that took her from me as a child and kept on taking her from me as a teenager and as an adult. She loved me fiercely; I never doubted that. But her illness made her less available—physically and emotionally—and while I know she never meant to hurt me, the impact of her lifelong illness did.

The details of just how hard those final weeks of my mom's life were, I shared with my closest friends.

"Did you know that chemo interacts with psych meds?" I'd ask them. I told them she was hallucinating again—something I hadn't seen in years. The chemo negated the effects of the meds, I told them, leaving her unable to stay present in this world. Now she was floating, full of fear, full of cancer and chemo, unable to walk to the bathroom or even sleep in peace for a few hours. I told them her eighty-year-old husband was dedicated and kind but exhausted, and I was flying back and forth with a new baby, sobbing in the airport.

I told them she refused to tell the doctor how sick she was and how much pain she was in. And I told them I was constantly returning to the house I grew up in, a place full of triggers and ghosts and pain, with my mother asking me, in the middle of the night, what I tell my parishioners facing a diagnosis like this—how I help them prepare to die. I told my friend that she would then cry and ask me to help her to the portable toilet at the foot of her bed, and then she'd yell that I wasn't responding fast enough, that I was hurting her. I told my friends that instead of putting the wipes covered in her shit into the toilet, she would fling them—like they were toxic waste—around the room until shit was on the carpet and walls. Another thing to fucking clean up, I would say, while she then slept and my fussing baby just calmed down and slept, when all I wanted was to sleep, too.

"You'll miss her," my colleagues would say. "This is big."

"Right," I said sometimes out loud to the people who knew the whole story. Right. I'll miss this. The flinging poop, the moans of pain, the nights where sleep is impossible between my crying six-month-old and my screaming mother. All I wanted was for this to be over, dear god, to be anywhere else but here.

Soon, this part of the journey was over. My mother died peacefully after settling into hospice care. We had a few long days together with the nurses washing her body and managing her pain. An afternoon where her best friends gathered round her bed, my mom unconscious but I swear listening in, as they told stories about their adventures together and her life. I let them talk and talk and talk, nursing my baby in the corner and asking questions here and there. We managed a funeral at the church where we grew up, honoring my mother's unconventional wishes as the organist played "Silent Night" in the middle of the service and the priest invited my mother to join Jesus and Elvis at the Welcome Table. We had people back to her house and the neighbors brought iced tea and whole hams and my brother insisted we serve the meal on the good china. My mother would have loved every minute of it.

My wife and kids and I drove back to New York late that night. I needed to leave—to get back to the life I'd created far from that place. I drove with a desperation I hadn't felt in years.

Back at home, with the caregiving and the sitting with suffering and all of the travel and triggers settling down, the portal opened. I welcomed it. I remembered the stories my mother's friends told, gathered around her bed that day in hospice. I imagined her the way they described her. I brought in the multiple truths of her life next to the old memories that haunted mine.

My mom was a teacher. She held a master's degree in early childhood education and alongside others brought Head Start to the city of Baltimore. She goofed off with her oldest friend all the time. She was widowed at an early age—her first husband, a musician and a photographer, dying from MS. She started again with my dad, letting her heart crack open to the possibility of their life together, and mine, too. She searched and searched for help with her illness, visiting a psychiatrist and consenting to treatment at a time when mental illness held a stigma that could have crushed her. She fought to stay here, to stay present, to be my mother, even when I pushed her away in some of the most painful ways possible.

All of this was true. Pushed up right next to the truth of the chaos and neglect and the doorway to abuse these things opened, there were other truths, too. She loved me fiercely. She was strong and resilient, resourceful and tenacious. She'd been dealt a shitty hand in so many ways, and she did not give up. Not even at the end when I wanted her to, when the pain seemed too great to me for her to continue. She fought to be here, to be part of my life, to love her grandchildren in a way she could never love me.

Back at home I felt the door of my heart loosening on its hinges as the story got more complex. Maybe it was because her mental illness couldn't hurt me anymore with all of its disappointments and pain. Maybe it was because as an adult and as a mother now myself, I could see that she was always more than my mom. She was a person with a whole life, of which I was only one part.

I never expected there would be a day when the first thought of my mother would be her strength. All my life, my first thoughts of her had been a video reel on repeat of terrifying times.

The days she showed up at school looking for me because she was lost.

The summer afternoon it was so hot, she started walking down the street taking her clothes off piece by piece, stepping naked into our neighbor's pool as I trailed behind pleading for her to stop.

The day she added something new to her repertoire and started talking in a different voice, convinced she was another person with another story and another life.

The night in the psych ward, this time with me as the patient, depression and rage overtaking me, as she begged for me to let her back in, saying she was better now and ready to be a parent. It's too late, I told her. You've missed too much, and I've gone too far. We could never have that relationship that she—and I—wanted. It was lost, though we did build something different in time.

It would be easier to put my relationship with my mom in an unchanging box. To freeze her in those harmful frames in my mind. But the portal pulled me then, as it does now, into possibility, and I want to follow. I want to let go of the baggage I no longer need. The judgment. I want my heart to soften to see the fullness of who my mother was and is, not just to me but to the world. I want to take up her resilience, her tenacity and resourcefulness and fierce love that found a way. I want my whole inheritance, not a simple story from the unchanging box.

I know I won't always get there gracefully. I won't always welcome the changes or turn to unlock the door on my way over the threshold. And I know that I'll never be able to do it on my own. I'll need to keep choosing the right and healing folks to trust, saying no to the things that don't work and yes to the things that will. I'll need to discover again and again that learning to love differently is hard—but the portal promises the worthy effort.

To Have without Holding

By Marge Piercy

Learning to love differently is hard,
love with the hands wide open, love
with the doors banging on their hinges,
the cupboard unlocked, the wind
roaring and whimpering in the rooms
rustling the sheets and snapping the blinds
that thwack like rubber bands
in an open palm.

It hurts to love wide open
stretching the muscles that feel
as if they are made of wet plaster
then of blunt knives, then
of sharp knives.

It hurts to thwart the reflexes
of grab, of clutch; to love and let
go again and again. It pesters
to remember the lover who is not in the bed,
to hold back what is owed to the work
that gutters like a candle in a cave
without air, to love consciously,
conscientiously, concretely, constructively.

TAKE WHAT YOU NEED

I can't do it, you say it's killing
me, but you thrive, you glow
on the street like a neon raspberry,
bright bachelor's button blue and bobbing
on the cold and hot winds of our breath,
As we make and unmake in passionate
diastole and systole the rhythm
of our unbound bonding, to have
and not to hold, to love
with minimized malice, hunger
and anger moment by moment balanced.

Chapter 11

Taking the Good...

It's often said that travel changes us, that experiencing other cultures and ways of doing things makes us more curious and more open. We aren't the same once we've seen the sun rise on a different shore. I tend to think the same thing is true once we start experiencing stories from different perspectives. The desire for complexity becomes contagious, and we find ourselves wanting to know more. Curiosity and an increasing sense of compassion for ourselves and others lead us to let go of the one-note versions of the stories that used to drive us, and we find ourselves searching for the whole story, our full inheritance, wherever we can.

When I was in seminary, I had a biblical studies professor who would pace in front of the class, translating sacred scripture from Hebrew and then Greek and then Latin as she walked back and forth, tossing in two or three different English versions of the text for good measure, teaching us in real time how much changing a word or a point of view could matter. Whole kingdoms, crusades, crucifixions, and systems of oppression had been based on those words. Whole lives could be lost or saved when someone new told the story.

Nine years after my mother's death, I found myself standing in the kitchen with my dad, doing dishes. He was in Minneapolis for a longer visit than usual, accomplishing one of the goals he'd set for himself when his cancer diagnosis surprised us all a few months earlier. Not knowing how long he had, he narrowed his hopes down to three things: he wanted to travel, to come visit me in Minnesota for more than our usual three days in the summer together, and to have one last great love affair.

I was honored to have made the list, even as I was devastated with the news. And there we were, together, in a seemingly mundane moment. We fell into a familiar rhythm, one I hadn't known since high school, with me washing and him drying. How many times had we done this when I was a kid? Standing at the sink with hands pruney from the dirty, soapy water, side by side getting the job done?

In just a few short months, my father had already done so much to prepare. Always the practical one, he started with getting his physical house in order. He made his will and health care directive, let us know what he wanted for a memorial service and where he wanted my brother and me to spread his ashes. We talked through where he wanted to die and who he wanted to take care of him if he got too sick to take care of himself. He had the windows replaced, arranged for the house to be painted, started sorting through his things.

I had been preparing, too. Reviewing memories, making plans, starting to let in the likelihood of a future without him in it. My dad's parents had lived into their eighties and nineties. This was all so different from what I had expected.

I thought about how he had separated from my mom my senior year of college. He waited until he was sure that I—the youngest—would launch before he finally pushed away, claiming for himself what was left of his life after twenty-five years of marriage, twenty-two of which were filled with the chaos of her mental illness and his trying to contain it.

He was forty-six when he left her—the same age I am now as I write. As the reality of my father's illness set in, I set my intentions for how I also wanted to be over these last few months together. What had I learned from my months with my mother that I could take with me on this unwanted journey?

We hadn't been close. There were short trips to see each other. And I'd come to help him with getting his house in order, cleaning, pitching old electronics long beyond use. Sometimes we'd talk on the phone—a challenge for two introverts with questionable social skills. In those first visits after his diagnosis, before he came to Minneapolis, he asked me the same question every time: what did he need to be doing to prepare for his death?

I thought about my mom, remembering how my heart softened after she died. I remembered the relief I felt letting more of her in. I liked how I changed as my story about her became more complex, grounded always in the truth of her love for me, even if she never could express it in a way I could fully receive.

With my dad, I hoped I could get to that softhearted place before he died so we could share that experience together in life. Soft heart, clear boundaries—that was the intention I set. I needed to pay attention to my own health—mental, physical, spiritual—as we navigated these next months together; that's where the clear boundaries came in. And standing side by side, doing the dishes together in our old familiar rhythm, I listened with a soft heart.

He started telling me about his older brother Teddy. The son my grandfather never got to meet—his son born and died before he returned from World War II. My grandparents never talked about Teddy or the war they'd both survived, how deep the loss cut. But my dad was talking now, telling me how Teddy had been sent away to the countryside of England like so many children during the bombing of London. And that Teddy died out there in the countryside, separated from his mother as she cowered in the bunkers below the burning streets. This was the hard story no one could talk about.

That was it for a while. My dad and I talked about the weather and his tickets on Southwest. We made breakfast for the kids. I lived those days with Emily Dickinson's poem sounding in my heart:

> Tell all the truth but tell it slant—
> Success in Circuit lies

I didn't want to push him away with my directness, but I wondered what other stories he had to tell. On the last morning of his more than three-day visit to Minneapolis, drinking coffee while the kids slept, I gathered my strength and invited him to go a little further.

"Are there stories about your life," I asked, "that you want to tell? Things you want to make sure that we know, so that years after your death I don't have to go searching to find out the important facts about our family?"

At first he hesitated. Then the floodgates opened—the truth coming out straight on, no longer slant.

One after another, he told stories of my mother's illness and what it meant for his life, and for ours. He talked about trying to care for her when he had no experience with mental illness and no idea what to do. How the experts he turned to couldn't help, his determination to protect her and us, as best he could.

He told me how he found out later that my mom's mother would come over during the day after he'd left for work—how she would take care of the house and us kids and my mom, how she'd start dinner and leave just before my father got home so that he would think everything was okay. She did this day after day, week after week, but she couldn't come all the time, and on those days the cracks would start to show.

He told me he didn't fully grasp what was going on until I was in preschool. My mother was teaching kindergarten at the church school I attended when he got a call from the priest. My mother had walked off, leaving her classroom full of students and me behind. He didn't know where she'd gone. A few hours later, my father received a second call. My mother was at the elementary school my brother attended, talking nonstop and cornering teachers in the hallway. A psychiatrist from the church stepped in and gave my mother some medicine to slow her down, but it didn't last for long.

Looking back, my father told me, there were signs, but no one knew how to read them. After my birth, for instance, my mother got it in her head that she couldn't come downstairs at the house. She stopped leaving her room and stopped interacting with everyone. Eventually, my father transitioned our life to the top floor, moving the dining room table upstairs so that we could have dinner together. Thinking about this later, I couldn't help but wonder if my mom's refusal to come downstairs played some part in their decision to move into a ranch house a year later, the home my mother would stay in for the rest of her life.

"The worst of it was never knowing what I'd come home to," my father said. I imagine him now at the age of twenty-five, with two kids and a wife he didn't know how to help. He had a job he loved, but he couldn't pour himself into it, always wondering what fresh hell would greet him when he walked through the door at the end of the day.

There, sitting side by side on the back deck of my Minneapolis home, he told me how much he wanted that first big job to turn into a career. He was an engineer in line for a promotion as plant manager. Every day, he'd work on drawings for the products the plant was creating. Every afternoon, he'd walk through the factory, seeing what people were making out of his drawings. He loved those afternoons on the factory floor until one day he was out walking around and heard his name being paged over the loudspeaker. His wife needed him to call home right away. It was a long walk back to his office, a long walk wondering what was unfolding at home. After that, he lost the promotion. He couldn't stay late at the office or get drinks with the boss. He arrived at nine and left at five.

My dad was seventy-two when we had this conversation. I knew he worried about money in retirement. Before our conversation, I thought of my father's lack of savings as a personality flaw: he couldn't manage to stay at the same job for long, and these were the consequences; it was that simple. He was always moving around from company to company when I was a kid, never making it long enough to get vested in the pension programs that were offered. I chalked this up as his fault.

But as he spoke, the story started to shift. My father couldn't stay at a job for long because he was busy taking care of all of us under impossible circumstances. Later in life he started his own business because it allowed him to work at home on his own flexible schedule. Maybe he was brilliant.

My softer heart began allowing me to see this both/and. These multiple truths. He kept on talking.

He told me how my brother and I would get dropped off with a friend or a neighbor or a family member when things got too hot at home. I remembered many of these drop-offs, but he filled in the details on a few. How one day he took us to a family friend's house for dinner and left us there for weeks. How on weekdays he'd drop me off at the neighbor's house at the top of the hill on his way to work so I wouldn't be home alone with my mom. I remembered what it felt like—the ease and the awkwardness of joining them in their well-oiled routine as we all sat down to breakfast together day after day, their family teaching me the glories of a regular breakfast and cheese melted on toast.

I remembered the afternoons when my grandmother would be standing in our door watching when I got off the bus. How relieved I felt when I saw her there, knowing I wouldn't be alone to manage whatever I'd find, knowing I could fold in and put my head on her soft chest, her arms wrapping around me, tucking me into her care.

I remembered the neighbors. The retired nurse at the end of the block. The old man across the street who laid out figurines on his lawn, moving them each day like a scavenger hunt created just for us. There must have been dozens of them—family and friends who took us in, neighbors that brought us home, teachers who kept an eye out. They never talked about what was going on, but each of them did what they could to keep us safe.

Maybe I've been good at collecting people who can help along the way. Maybe my family has been, too. Maybe I learned it from them.

Somehow, with all of the chaos that was our lives, my father managed to help me with homework and take me to softball practice. As we talked,

I thanked him for that sacrifice. He teared up for the first time.

"There was nowhere else I'd rather be," he said. "Your games in those random small towns in Pennsylvania—that was exactly where I wanted to be."

We moved inside after that, each of us needing a breather to wipe our eyes and settle ourselves. Our British roots and training in emotional constipation required a pause in the action.

Sitting on the couch in our living room, the conversation continued. "I've gone over it in my head for years," he said. "Wondering if I did the right thing by you kids by staying. I think I did the right thing. I hope I did the right thing."

We hadn't talked like this in years, and here he was, offering up an opportunity for forgiveness, for reassurance, for peace. He opened the door. And I moved through it, grateful for the invitation.

"I think you're right, Dad. I don't think there was anything else you could have done. You did the best you could in a really hard situation. You did the best you could to keep us safe, to keep things calm. You did everything you could."

Saying this out loud, I knew it was true. He had sacrificed his career, his hopes for himself, his chance at lifelong love that could love him back. He had done everything he could, and still I got hurt. Assuring him did not mean negating my own pain.

All of these things could be true at the same time: He had done all that he could, and it had helped. And it hadn't been enough to protect me entirely. I still had anger and pain and wishes for how things could have gone differently. And now I had gratitude, too, and an understanding that I was loved—so very loved. The story was getting more complex. Soft heart and clear boundaries leading the way.

Chapter 12

. . . And Taking the Bad

My wife used to say that the hardest part about looking back on her previous relationship was recognizing all of the ways that she had contributed to her own diminishment. It stung to realize she had stifled the spark in her that knew that something wasn't right. She kept denying the truth that her still small voice dared to speak until it got quieter and quieter and barely spoke at all.

I'm always amazed at the power of family systems to reinforce the status quo. Keeping things stable and steady seems to be our most desired state, even when the way things are is hurting us all. We see this in our country with the grip of systemic oppression, and it happens, too, in our workplaces and our homes. The people in power and sometimes the powerless, too, choose the way things are rather than taking the risk of hoping for something better. It's not so easy to step through the portals with curiosity, carrying little luggage, believing that another world is possible and fighting for it, too.

Growing up, the status quo was simple. The highest good in my house centered on keeping my mother calm. Any little thing could upset her, throwing the rest of us into chaos as we tried to simultaneously care for her and keep everything together on the outside. To let anyone know just how bad it was at home meant the flimsy scaffolding we had built would come crashing down. No one questioned this arrangement.

Early on I learned to take the list to the grocery store, carrying the already signed check my mother had given me, filling out the numbers for the total at the register. The clerk at the Safeway knew my mother's cigarette order, and at only two miles away, I could walk there whenever she ran out. I could cook a meal from whatever I found in the fridge, as long as there was a can of tomatoes to cover it all up. The daily trips to the nurse's office at school stopped as soon as they suggested I see a doctor. Unspoken and spoken rules in my family removed the possibility. Breaking them meant breaking my family, breaking my mother, shattering our world.

Somewhere along the way, all of this became normal. Rules that others would immediately question had become commonplace, unquestionable to me. I could understand how this happened when I was a kid, stuck in a system I didn't create. But as I got older, it happened again. And then again.

A job that started off hopeful turned toxic. Something was off from the beginning, but I pushed it down, eager for the work and an eye attuned to what could go right. I stayed in my first marriage for years longer than I probably should have, ignoring the clear signals we were both sending about the very different futures we wanted. Still I continued on. At work and at home, I stuffed down sign after sign, not wanting to rock the boat, not wanting to take the risk to begin again.

You can only hold the status quo for so long, looking for the best in the situation, capitalizing on what you can, averting your gaze from the truth. Following the rules of these unhealthy systems only works until some lines get crossed, and then there is a decision to make. The lines can feel dramatic, but there are always signs and signals along the way.

Growing up, there were certainly signals along the way that something wasn't quite right and that holding it all in was hurting me. The cracks showed in the way I saw the world. My father and brother and I were bound together in an unspoken pact to care for my mother at home no matter what. By the age of eight, I could smile through almost anything. I could cook and clean and comfort someone suffering from severe mania or depression without batting an eye. But even I couldn't dip my dinner spoon into a bowl full of bugs without hesitating.

It started off looking like a promising night. My mom cooked dinner instead of leaving it to me, and she'd gone all out. She'd made crab soup—an expensive delicacy in our house—and she'd had it simmering in the crockpot all afternoon. The house smelled great.

We sat down at the table and my mom dished up the dinner. Steaming red broth with all my favorite vegetables and little morsels of crab meat filled the bowls, along with a layer of spices settling on the surface.

They weren't spices, though.

The cupboards at our house were a minefield. Any open container quickly became the territory of the bugs. Keeping the house clean and managing what could have been typical infestations of bugs in the flour, or fleas on the cat, or regular cleaning of the bathroom, all of these were well outside the bounds of what was possible at our house. So I learned to work around what I could. I ate mostly out of cans or the freezer—the safe zone. I avoided the spices and the baking supplies because you couldn't always tell what you were going to get.

The worst bugs were the tiny ones. You could mistake them for poppyseeds or celery seeds. Until you saw them move through the flour, you thought you were mixing in something magnificent. Now minuscule wings floated on top of the broth. Later in life, I'd come to know the fancy toppings that could be served on top of soup—crème fraîche, a swirl of herb oil, croutons—but that's not what this was.

When my mom got up to serve herself, I leaned over to my dad and whispered, "There are bugs in the soup."

He looked down at his bowl and then back up at me. "Eat the soup," he said.

This request seemed impossible. I don't know why this was the time I spoke up, but I said it again.

"Mom," I began gently, "I think there are bugs in the soup."

"Oh," she said, looking down, her confidence clearly wavering from the pride we saw just moments before. "It's just some celery seed," she said. But she looked uncertain.

"Dig in," my father announced as he scooped deep into his bowl and took a bite. "Definitely celery seed in there. Delicious choice, Shirley." He looked squarely at me, telegraphing his earlier message: *Eat the damn soup. Now.*

"If it's celery seed," I wondered out loud, "then why do they have wings?"

My father glared at me. I was breaking the rules. The rules that said we kept our mouths shut about unsettling things at all costs. The rule that said we suck it up and smile.

I was breaking the rules, and for a second it felt like I was breaking the entire ordered world. I took a deep breath. If I continued to assert myself, it could mean chaos. She would dump the soup out and cry. She'd lock herself in the bedroom and my father would beg her to open the door, finally having to force his way in.

Was it worth it?

Something in me shifted. I ate the bugs, but for the first time I knew that keeping the peace was a higher value than my own well-being. That the rules were toxic to me. And that I couldn't count on my father to confirm my reality publicly if it meant upsetting my mother and upsetting the system. I learned that night that I would always say yes.

Years after I'd left the house and established myself on my own, I would start to tell the truth, breaking the family rules and again feeling like I was breaking the world. It was only when the fresh start I'd worked so hard to establish by leaving for college got threatened that I started to risk breaking the world open in earnest. Only when my sobriety, my survival, demanded that I start letting go of the old rules did the toxic system begin to release its grip on my life.

There were so many old rules to sort through. And so many to discard.

For those whose lives were sacrificed on the altar of their family's well-being, there was nothing too sick to stomach. No reason good enough not to keep your mouth shut. No limit to what you would do or what you could take to protect the people you love.

And when you broke these rules, even your allies would betray you.

From this mess, I began to reach past the buggy surface to the sustenance beneath, writing new rules that serve me still.

When the fire hit, it felt like our whole world went flying apart. Distraught, I fell back into the familiar grip of the old rules at times—trying to carry too much, keeping my mouth shut as I scrambled to make it all look good on the outside.

Thank god for the practice of years and the people who would not let me go. Thank god for the ones who reminded me to take the risk to tell the truth, who kept me company in the narrow places I wasn't sure I could pass through. Thank god for that still small voice demanding my survival that kept speaking up even when I felt the world would break if I said words that were true.

Here are my new rules, the rules I've been learning ever since bug-bowl days:

- Tell the truth even when it hurts, even when it is complicated.
- Keep good company, with allies who are able to hear the truth, who ask for it.

- Be willing to disrupt the status quo in service of the truly greater good.
- You clear away the wreckage of the past when you put your own health first, when you trust that from that centered place, you can serve others in ways that heal yourself and the others you intend to serve.

Even now I still wonder, How much is too much to give for someone you love? When does sacrifice turn from sacred to sacrilege? Where is the line between coercion and choice, between free will and no other way out? Will feeling virtuous save you when you look back wondering if you did what you could as death comes in close? And how will I know when I've given up too much or sacrificed just enough?

Some answers are clear now. Would I eat a bowl of bugs to keep my mother out of the hospital?

Maybe I did it once, but no, not again.

Chapter 13

Taking Time

Early on in my recovery from alcoholism, the simplistic slogans constantly repeated in recovery meetings nearly sent me screaming. Sayings like "One day at a time," "This too shall pass," and "Think, think, think" seemed so stupid I could hardly bear it. Cross-stitched, hanging next to the coffee pot in almost every recovery room, these sayings seemed to mock me. Did they think I was stupid? Did I not know that one day at a time actually added up to not drinking for the rest of your life? Of course all things passed. And thinking, well, that only got me in trouble.

One sponsor I met with for several years ended every conversation we had with a slogan. It was infuriating. This super serene woman would listen to me rant and struggle, and then she'd remind me to pray and sign off with recovery program jargon.

One day I called her from my car, pulled over in the parking lot of the corner grocery store. I was sitting there sobbing, my newborn son strapped into his car seat behind me. I'd gone to visit a new friend, another mother with a young baby, and our short time together had undone me. This new friend had welcomed me into her clean house and chatted happily while her kid played peacefully on the floor. She offered me fresh-baked scones and chattered on about her child's sleep routine and how much fun she was having being a mom.

My beloved son hadn't once slept through the night since he was born. Our house was a mess. My wife and I were working opposite shifts to avoid day care. We were exhausted. As I listened to my friend, I kept trying to settle down my insistently unsettled boy. Thirty minutes in, I looked for my exit.

I couldn't have felt worse. As soon as I could, I packed us up and left. I pulled over into the nearest parking lot and let the hot tears flow.

My sponsor listened for a while, and then, on cue, she recited a slogan.

"Don't worry," she said. "This too shall pass. For you and for her."

It took me a minute to understand what she had just said. So she elaborated: "This too shall pass, Jen. Your exhaustion, his inability to sleep, your messy house. And this too shall pass for her, too. Her perfect days, her sleep-filled nights, her homemade scones. This too shall pass, for her and for you. It always does." I began laughing through my tears. Those slogans might have something in them for me after all.

In the first weeks after our house fire, my spiritual director cautioned me against trying to make sense of things too soon. "You need to let it all unfold before you can know what it will mean for you," she told me. "Don't rush it." I heard a recovery slogan in her words—time takes time, she seemed to be saying. Time doesn't heal all wounds, and time alone cannot fix things like magic. And I heard those words in a new way, and time did show me how we can heal.

The year that my house burned down, I experienced an unexpected blessing. The minister who had held my position before me had retired just before I arrived, and she was still in town. She had told me she couldn't support the church she loved in the ways that she was used to. But she could support me, she said. And she did. She now had time. With that time, she showed up to sort through the boxes from the restoration company, to pick through the insulation in search of the jewelry that had gone flying from our dressers, to polish the passed-down silver from my grandmother that we pulled out of the buffet. In so many ways she was there for me, offering time, but she also offered me poetry.

When it was time to move back home after our fire, my clergy friends gathered to bless our house for our family's return. Each of them brought poems and prayers, talismans and stones to encircle us in safety. She brought words adapted from this poem by Karen Benke:

Not Without Longing

Come, rest
inside this house
you left to travel
so far. Home now,
the braided rope of the past
no longer anything
you must look for or save.
The heart, left open
will heal itself
as a new moon rises.

She must have really thought I needed this poem because she gave it to me on several occasions. In fact, it's all over my house—tucked inside the bread box, nestled in my morning meditation manual, scrawled out on a reused scrap of paper, placed neatly in a packet of poems in my bedside table.

Maybe it was the "rest inside this house" that she wanted for me. Maybe it was the feeling of "home now." And maybe it was the reminder of the most trustworthy rule I've ever known, that as much as it hurts, "the heart left open will heal itself as a new moon rises."

When I was twelve years old, a whole lot of hard things happened. Among the most physically challenging was when my appendix ruptured. Quickly, I became very ill. By the time I got to surgery, I was in so much pain that I'd given up caring what would happen next. An infection had spread through my insides at a surprising rate, the full extent of which wasn't known until the surgeon cut into me on the table. The best hope for my recovery, I was later told, was to leave the wound open, allowing it to heal, hopefully, from the inside out.

I'd never heard of anything like this before, but nurses came in like clockwork, irrigating the wound and changing the bandages. A tube down my nose removed everything it could from my stomach, and the nurses washed away all they could from the outside. The forces of clearing and cleaning, of hoped-for healing, were applied from all directions. And my body began to work again, to return me to health.

While I was recovering, I never looked down at the open wound. It only took one time of watching my brother lose his lunch when he accidentally wandered into my room during the changing of the bandage to figure out I didn't need to. It wasn't until I'd been home for a week that I dared to lift up my shirt and look—the angry red scar going this way and that, one straight line stretching from belly button to pubic bone and another going perpendicular to make what looked like an upside-down T on my lower belly. The scar was huge, but it had already closed. My body was healing itself from the inside out.

For years, I paid more attention to the events leading up to that surgery than the miracle of my healing. I wondered what would have happened if my illness had been tended to sooner and why we didn't realize its seriousness until I was so, so sick. I forgot, for a time, how my father sat with me in my hospital room, holding my hand, reading me stories, fixing that nasogastric tube that was constantly losing suction and waking me up with its incessant beeping. At the time, he was working for a medical supply company, working with so many of the machines that kept me alive in that time. Sitting by my side, he'd silence their alarms and fix the machines, letting me slide back into sleep.

When I finally went home, my friends were waiting for me. They helped me outside, walking me to the street corner where they could sneak me a cigarette—the first I'd had in weeks. That year when so much was going wrong, when my grandmother had died my body had found a way to survive, healing itself from the inside out.

If a body could do all that, then maybe, just maybe, a heart could, too.

And time would take time. And the tools would be different—recovery from alcoholism instead of surgery for sepsis, counseling instead of antibiotics, exercise and massage to reconnect me with my body, and tears and tears and more tears to wash the wounds inside and out. If I could just hold my heart open, letting the infection clear out and the love pour in, perhaps my heart might just heal itself from the inside out, too.

I wish that the poet promised that the heart left open would heal quickly and forever, but what she writes is this: "The heart, left open will heal itself as a new moon rises." Promising that the journey goes on, that we will break open again and again, and the heart—resilient and strong—will heal itself with each turning cycle of life.

I've always liked to move fast, wishing for one-and-done healing. For speed even if it means pain, to know what to expect and precisely when the hurting will stop. Because I've often been "rewarded" for this kind of behavior, I then applied the Time Doesn't Take Time mindset to healings, and it hasn't worked too well. When I go too fast, I tend to hurt myself, physically and emotionally. Time takes time, I now say to myself, even when I don't want it to.

My hardest job is not to rush. To keep letting the love in. To say yes to help when it is offered. To experience and trust and maybe even rest in the web of support that keeps on holding us. My job is to let it all in, all that I can of the pain and the care.

My job is to notice the way my eight-year-old comforted my five-year-old, the way my wife turned to me with kindness, and the way the two of us carried each other through in those months after the fire. My job is to weep when I need to, to keep my heart open so it can heal itself from the inside out.

One day at a time, our bodies and spirits do what they know how to do, knitting the broken places back together with scars that are stronger than the skin and muscle that held us before.

Chapter 14

Take Courage

In the early days of my sobriety, I had a hard time understanding why so many people were showering me with their time and care and attention, inviting me out to coffee or joining me for my daily ice-cream habit. They kept an eye on me and shepherded me around, helping me stay on track.

In those first days, I remember telling my sponsor that I didn't think I was worth all this, that soon all these kind people would see me for who I really was, and they'd drop me like a ton of bricks. I remember the fierce look in her face, how she stopped and stared at me.

"Do you really think we are *all* stupid?" she asked. "Do you think you are so smart you're fooling us, that we're so dumb we couldn't see through you the moment we met you? All of us? We know you, Jen Crow," she said, "and we love you. You aren't fooling anyone. You have surrounded yourself with smart, thoughtful people, and we will love you until you can love yourself."

That someone else could love you until you could love yourself was something completely new to me. And those friends taught me that you can borrow faith, too. You can trust someone else's clarity when you cannot trust your own. You can borrow love, can even hold on to someone else's hope, until you can find it for yourself again.

Twenty years later—two marriages, two kids, and a house fire behind me—I asked my therapist a similar question. "Why do you do this work with me?" I wondered out loud. "Why do you take my phone calls, answer my emails, look at me with that calm gaze of love?"

"You're a good investment," she said simply, smiling.

For months after the fire, her words fueled me. When I couldn't trust that I would take the turn out of this crisis, I could trust that this wise one saw something in me that I could not see in myself. I could hold on to her hope when the bad dreams came and the nights stretched out forever, the memories flying through like unwelcome ghosts. I could match my breath to hers, slowing down my heart rate and allowing the oxygen to wash through and soothe my body.

In college, my artist-philosopher girlfriend once shared her understanding of time with me. What if time wasn't linear, she wondered, but instead each moment was like a slide—a second captured in stillness—and life was all those slides stacked up on top of each other, with us looking through, the moments and images bleeding one into the other forward and back and us, holding it all, knowing it all, containing it all? That's where déjà vu comes from, she posited, and clairvoyance. It's all already there; it's just that some of us can see through the slides sideways, let the light in in a way that opens the whole of our experience up to us at once.

While I'm not sure I completely agree with this idea of time, considering its possibility has changed me. Nearly thirty years later, I'm still thinking about it, wondering what might be possible just outside the edges of my imagination. And I do think sometimes others can see through our stack of slides and hold the fullness of our stories for us when we feel stuck.

It's easy for me to accept that all of us experience things differently. My son is color-blind, so when we look at the same object, we see different things. And my brother and I had the same parents but different childhoods. Add in age and developmental stages, worldviews and experiences, education and exposure to difference or a nontypically working mind— we will never experience things exactly alike. As my heart softens and my mind opens further, I wonder if maybe there is more to the stories I thought were set in stone. I wonder which ones I haven't examined yet. Maybe I can understand things anew, shine a side light into the stack of slides and meet a new understanding that can change the way I understand my life, can change the way I live.

Growing up, I often wondered when it was that my mom first got sick. Asking around, I heard this story: My mother's first major break with reality happened when I was born. Something in her snapped. She retreated into her room and into herself. She couldn't take care of me, wouldn't pick me up. Her second major break happened when I started school. With me no longer home to help her stay tethered to this world, she wandered off in her mind and left us again.

Hearing the facts this way at a young age, I told myself a story. My birth brought on my mother's illness. I caused it. There was something so wrong with me that even as an infant, I had the power to destroy the one person I needed the most. As I got older, I told myself the next logical iteration of the story. If I had caused my mother's mental illness, then maybe I had the power to cure it, too. I at least had to try.

It wasn't until I was much older that I learned there were other ways to tell this story. There was the reality of postpartum psychosis to consider. College classes and the psychology section of the library showed me that mental illness like my mother's couldn't be caused by another person and couldn't be cured by them, either. Signs early on in my parents' marriage pointed to something else at work alongside the idyllic illusion of a perfect family with one boy and one girl—king's choice, my father would call it—in those 1970s suburbs. There was the teaching I took in at my new-to-me church in my twenties, taking out the story of original sin that supported my childhood understanding of myself as foundationally flawed and putting in its place the possibility that every child, including this one, was born whole and holy and worthy, loved and lovable—one more redeemer in this world.

If I hadn't caused my mother's illness and I could not cure it, then all of a sudden my life could look a whole lot different. My purpose on this earth might reach beyond my nuclear family. I might not have to sacrifice myself to an unwinnable cause. Another world might be possible.

The stories we tell ourselves and each other matter. A new piece of information, a turn of the kaleidoscope of perception, and the story shifts. Possibilities we never dreamed of emerge.

I know that letting go of our stories is not simple and that writing and accepting new ones is not easy, especially if we have been held captive for some time or have felt safe in our old ways of understanding. There can be a lot of unraveling to do as we unlearn the lies or the overly simple truths that used to guide us. We can feel exposed and vulnerable as the fortress we built around ourselves opens up to the air. We might be afraid of what we will lose. We might be afraid of shaking up the status quo and welcoming the new life a new story might bring. And writing and rewriting our stories can hurt—but it can also make our lives our own.

We know that the fires of life will come and keep coming. We know that we will lose people and things that matter. It happens when relationships shift, when illness strikes, when a job ends or a cycle in our lives turns. It happens again and again. The question is not if the fires will come but what we will do with them, and what stories we will tell ourselves and each other. This life is ours to make, ours to live and give back in all of the ways we choose. Our complicated, complex, ever-changing stories are ours to write.

We also know humans are a good investment, we doubt-filled, broken, beautiful, flawed, and creative creatures. We can hold on to each other, trusting in the heart's ability to heal itself. We can turn to the generations that have lived and died, bearing witness to the story's power to imagine and write new ways of being into existence.

Weeks before the bolt of lightning that blew up our lives, I got a new tattoo: a giant watercolor phoenix. I'd been dreaming about that tattoo for ages, and it finally felt like time. My life was my own. I was settled and satisfied, happy in my marriage, crushing it in my career. After years of therapy and sobriety, I was reclaiming my body, too. This tattoo would cover up the last visible scar from my cutting days as a teenager and young adult. The ink would mark my body as healed and healing. This tattoo would go with me everywhere I went, reminding me of who I was and what I could do.

A phoenix. A work of art. Rising from the ashes of experiences that could have killed me, I am here—beautiful and flowing, I will rise.

In the days after the fire, the irony of it kept me laughing. A phoenix tattoo. For real. You can't make this shit up.

But there it was, and there it is, and thank god for that tattoo—a daily reminder of who I am and what I can do. The power of the past helping me to heal instead of harm this time.

Thanks to the past, I knew that hardship did not have the power to determine the shape of my life. I had that power. The story was written on my arm. I knew that it would hurt like hell, and it would take longer than I wanted, but we would heal. That even with all of our possessions gone, we had so much. We had humor and hope. We had a community that cared and would not let us go.

When the nights got long and I wondered how I could live, I remembered with gratitude that we all walked out of that house. Resilience was already a part of my story. I could rely on that muscle anytime, trusting that some part of me already knew the way through this, to that next future I couldn't yet imagine.

My whole life I've been asking how it is that some people survive horrible experiences and some do not. I've studied psychology and theology, read myself into the world of fantasy and dreams searching for the ancient alchemical formula that transforms shit into gold. There are all kinds of theories and all kinds of stories that take us traveling along on the hero's journey. Here's mine: Maybe a little bit of love can accomplish more than any strategy or treatment plan. Maybe a heart left open will heal itself again and again. Maybe it's resilience. Good company, imagination, and willingness. Maybe it's strength or luck or time doing what it can do. Maybe there's more than we can comprehend with our limited human understanding.

Whatever fires of life have come your way, you are stronger than you know, and you can survive more than you think you can bear. You may not be able to imagine a way through right now, but like others have held hope for me, I can hold the hope for you. We can take turns holding each other up and cheering each other on. You're a good investment. And chances are good that if you've lived this long, you already possess the foundation of resilience. I hope you find your way.

Whether you are here searching for hope for yourself or someone else, here—take my courage, borrow my faith, let in my love. I've been given so much. I have plenty to spare.

Chapter 15

Take the Turn

Several times a week, I lie on my back in the basement of our rebuilt house, looking up at the rafters and the wires, the HVAC vents and the water and gas lines. I'm lying there in Savasana, the final resting pose of my yoga practice—my back on the mat, my body rooted to the ground in the strangely named corpse pose—breathing, feeling, shaking and crying some days, resting and giving thanks on others. Every time I lie there, I look up and I'm bathed in brightness, exposed light bulbs and white paint everywhere above and around me. It's a long way from the bathroom floor where this story began.

After the fire, after Dumpster Day and demolition, a crew came through and covered all that remained.

They sprayed layer after layer of this special white paint on the rafters and the wires, the remaining HVAC and water and gas lines, encapsulating all that was left. The paint contained the damage, the smell of smoke locked in tight underneath all of those layers. The basement is the only place you can still see it—the way the house looked after the fire, the story of its resurrection told through shiny silver HVAC runs, wood recently added to reinforce the floors, and bright white paint.

If you didn't know about the lightning and were seeing the house for the first time, you'd never know we had a fire. It's been long enough that nothing looks new. The wood floors are scratched, there's a nick in the granite countertop, and the furniture we bought finally feels like our own. The kids' clothes are everywhere, their wet towels in a heap on their bedroom carpet. The basement storage area that looked so bare when we moved back home is awkwardly full again. The to-do list of repairs and home improvements has plenty on it. We've been lucky enough to live through four Christmases, four summers, four back-to-schools— long enough that we know now what we have and what we don't, no new surprises lurking around the corner.

It's a beautiful house now. A hundred-year-old bungalow in South Minneapolis, it appears small from the street. Three bedrooms, two and a half bathrooms, a finished basement, and an office; an open kitchen, a first-floor master suite, a den, and a full bathroom on the second floor along with the kids' bedrooms. So much room for two parents, two kids, and two dogs. So much nicer than it was when we bought it.

We painted the front door red to match our window boxes. The rebuilt chimney stands tall, brick by tedious brick put back in place above the new roof where the fire shot through. There's a mural of clouds on the ceiling of that room now, the phrase "The journey of a million miles begins with a single step" painted there, a special request from our son.

Every spring since we got home, my wife plants flowers in the yard. Roses, lilies, hydrangeas, and hostas spread out like wildfire, their sprouts poking up in new places each year. The lilac tree outside our window gets fuller all the time. This summer, we cleared the boulevard and put in a butterfly garden. Raised beds and a squash patch took over half the front yard. I know each plant as a symbol of energy we have to give. Our neighbors probably just wish we'd stop.

Lying on my back, I can still see it—the way the house looked in those first days after the fire. The bright white paint covering everything. Wires and wood exposed. The bones of the place visible, the nervous system and connective tissue. It's all there under the new walls and windows and roof. The house left open to heal itself. The pain and the struggle, the rebirth and the rebuilding hidden from view for the outside world. You have to come in close for the rafters and the wires to tell the story.

Early on after we returned home, we'd catch a whiff of the smoke smell and the nightmare would descend upon us. Panic, loss, fear. Breath I chased but could not catch. We wondered if we could stay, if we'd have to sell the house we'd put all we had into, if the smell would ever go away. Some days we wondered if it was even real. I don't know when it stopped, but the smell doesn't come around anymore. My kids light a candle at dinner as we say our prayers and fight to blow it out when the meal is done. They want to watch the smoke and play with the wax. It's only me now that flinches at the fire.

Lying on my back in the basement, I wonder if it will always be this way, and I know now that it won't. As uncomfortable as I can still get, I know that this too shall pass. That time takes time, and that change will happen one day at a time. After all, I'm doing yoga on our basement floor, and no one could have predicted that. I can trust that change will keep coming—good and bad—because god knows I didn't see that lightning coming, or this friendship or that job or this wild love.

As the kids and the dogs wander through this tucked-away corner of the basement I've carved out for myself, checking in and nudging me with their wet noses when I try to settle into silence, I remember that I am never alone, even when I want to be. Friends and family and construction workers of all kinds will keep showing up when my house or my heart breaks. They will do for me what I cannot do for myself. Holding on to hope, spray-painting the ceiling, putting up the walls. It will never be just me and my backpack again. It never really was.

I've learned I can tell the story of the fire so many ways. I could talk about the unfairness of it all—lightning in the middle of the night? Are you kidding? What are the chances of that?

I could talk about the insurance company and wonder why they would pay for this and not that. Why they insisted the second-floor bathroom, just feet from the fire, could stay intact while the basement was a total loss. I could remember the way it all went out the door, insurance adjustors stepping on bedtime books and busting up Lego creations as they assessed the damage, my dog-eared library and our journals, pictures, poetry, precious minutiae we only knew through its absence—all of it swept up and out the door into the dumpster.

I could talk about the tears and the 2:00 a.m. wake-ups that still startle me. The house we can hardly afford.

I could talk about our dog who huddles in the corner of the yard and refuses to come in when we change the batteries in the smoke alarm. I could tell you how my daughter hates it when I go away, each of us a little bit scared that something unpredictable like a bolt of lightning will separate us and I won't return. I could tell you how my son still holds on to his size-four shoes, the ones he wore when we all walked out of that house. All of these things are true.

And I can tell you how we never wanted for a place to stay or food to eat. I can tell you how our friends and family and friends who are family, our community, came forward to make sure we had everything we'd need. The classmates at school who brought in books, the author from church who called on all of her children's-book-writing friends and the package upon package of autographed books that arrived for our kids, filling their shelves with wonder and love from around the world. I could tell you about the woman who barely knew me who put a fifty-dollar bill in my hand that first day when I didn't know which end was up, how just before her husband died two years later it was me who heard his confession and then laid him to rest, taking my turn to comfort her the best way I knew how. I could tell you how people came through, how things worked out, how my family turned in toward each other with kindness and care.

I can tell you that the heart left open will heal itself. The story can be told this way and that way. And all of it is true. We can hold it all.

I could tell you that one of the early gifts we received from the unknown angels at church who refused to follow my minimalist plan was a yoga mat, gray with light-green flowers—the one I lie on still, looking up at the bright white paint on the rafters.

NOTES

Introduction
"A Theology Adequate for the Night": Nancy Shaffer, *Instructions in Joy*

Chapter 2
"We think we tell stories, but stories often tell us": Rebecca Solnit, *The Faraway Nearby*

Chapter 3
"One of the reasons people cling to their hates": James Baldwin, *The Fire Next Time*

Chapter 5
"Ours is not the task of fixing the entire world all at once": Dr. Clarissa Pinkola Estés, "Letter to a Young Activist During Troubled Times"

Chapter 9
"Inescapable network of mutuality, tied in a single garment of destiny": Martin Luther King Jr., "Letter from a Birmingham Jail"

Chapter 10

"We can choose to walk through it": Arundhati Roy, *Azadi: Freedom. Fascism. Fiction*

"To Have Without Holding": Marge Piercy, *The Moon Is Always Female*

Chapter 11

"Tell all the truth but tell it slant— / Success in Circuit lies": Emily Dickinson, *The Poems of Emily Dickinson: Reading Edition*

Chapter 13

"Not Without Longing": Karen Benke, *Sister*

SOMETHING TO TAKE WITH YOU

Chapter Resources and Additional Reading

The Quaker author Parker Palmer teaches about the importance of using a "third thing" to approach the tender and often shy places in our lives:

"In Western culture, we often seek truth through confrontation. But our headstrong ways of charging at truth scare the shy soul away. If soul truth is to be spoken and heard, it must be approached 'on the slant.'"

We can approach the soul "on the slant" by using both intentionality and indirection. Intentionality means we bring our focus to the important topic at hand; indirection asks us to explore the topic metaphorically, through myth, music, art, story, poetry, movement—anything that invites the deeper places in us to notice and respond. A "third thing" can be anything that has its own story: poems, paintings, parks, memoirs, research, slogans. Anything that tells the truth about something that matters to us, offering us a mediated way to experience and respond.

Reading has always been a way for me to explore new ideas, possibilities, and places at my own pace, all from the safety of my particular surroundings. Here, I offer up a few of the "third things" and sources for learning that have shaped me, trusting that you will use them in the best way for you in this moment, perhaps approaching them like I did with the suggestions in *Living Sober*—exploring them on your own or in a group, noticing what draws your interest and offers support for further study or healing, leaving behind what doesn't help, and adding your own notes, poems, and quotes in the margins.

The Stories That Shape Us, the Stories We Write

James Baldwin's classic, *The Fire Next Time*, is part memoir and part political manifesto, an essential work of literature that helped galvanize the civil rights movement. Baldwin's book shows how our individual and communal stories interact with and affect each other, how the personal is political and the political is personal.

All of Rebecca Solnit's books focus on stories in some way, and each one of them has lessons to teach about the importance of how we focus our attention and the narratives we write, accept, or leave unexamined. In particular, *The Faraway Nearby*, *Hope in the Dark*, and *A Paradise Built in Hell* all offer stories and frameworks full of examples of how the stories that shape us can direct our lives.

This Bridge Called My Back: Writings by Radical Women of Color shares foundational writings of resistance, sharing commitments to new ways of listening and including all of our stories, so that we can write a more life-giving story for us all.

In her book *Unapologetic: A Black, Queer, and Feminist Mandate for Radical Movements*, theologian Charlene Carruthers invites us into frameworks for liberation that can shift, support, and expand the ways we understand our stories and the stories of our communities.

Through poetry and essays, Mary Oliver shares stories of attention, focusing on nature and the inner workings of her own spirit. In particular, *Upstream* and *Long Life* offer essays that can help us use Oliver's observations and reflections as a prism for our own.

In the dedication to his autobiography, *With Head and Heart*, the theologian Howard Thurman shares the story of a stranger who helped him as a boy and changed the trajectory of his life forever. The stories continue, offering us a window into the life experiences that shaped him and his writing, which in turn shaped so many others and the trajectory of our nation.

In the book *Jesus and the Disinherited*, Thurman writes specifically for those who are "living with their backs against the wall," sharing new interpretations of the stories of Jesus that have supported everyday individuals and prophets like Dr. Martin Luther King Jr. in their quest for personal and social worth, dignity, and essential human rights.

How we tell the stories of our times matters. Arundhati Roy offers a shift in perspective that can be liberatory not only for our understanding and approach to the COVID-19 pandemic but also to the key moments in our lives in her essay "The Pandemic Is a Portal" and the collection that contains it, *Azadi: Freedom. Fascism. Fiction.*

Grief

Grief is usually what brings people into my office at church. People don't come to see their clergyperson when things are going well—though we'd certainly welcome more of those conversations! No, people reach out when there is nowhere else to go. When a loved one is dying or has died, when someone is faced with a new diagnosis or a terminal prognosis, when it's time to plan a memorial service, or two or twenty years have passed since their loss and they are still working out how to go on.

I keep a short list of books and poems to recommend nearby at all times; too many can be overwhelming. Here are a few.

Thirst by Mary Oliver, a collection of poems written after the death of the poet's life partner that captures so many of the feelings and experiences of grief and healing through metaphor and magic. If a whole book of poetry is too much, go right to "Heavy"—this poem alone can carry you for a time.

When Things Fall Apart by Pema Chödrön, short Western Buddhist meditations and teachings that offer stories and techniques for living with change and loss—and the impermanence in everyday living.

John O'Donohue's *To Bless the Space between Us: A Book of Blessings*, a book for almost all occasions that also manages to recognize the particularity of individual moments, such as "For Broken Trust,"

"For the Breakup of a Relationship," and "For a New Beginning," just to name a few.

Written after the unexpected death of her husband and creative partner, *The Cure for Sorrow: A Book of Blessings for Times of Grief* by Jan Richardson offers blessings and prayers that put into words what we so often think but too rarely say while honoring the complexity of our feelings and experiences in times of grief and loss. You can also stay connected to more of Richardson's writings through her website, paintedprayerbook.com.

If you want to come in sideways, through fiction, *Afterlife* by Julia Alvarez offers insight into the many ways we experience grief and how we can carry our loved ones with us in the best of ways even after they are physically gone from us.

If you want to go further with the words of Nancy Shaffer, author of the poem "A Theology Adequate for the Night"—which alone has carried me through many dark nights of the soul—she also chronicled her experiences with illness, mortality, and life in her last year in her book *While There is Still Light: Writing from a Minister Facing Death*.

Francis Weller's *The Wild Edge of Sorrow: Rituals of Renewal and the Sacred Work of Grief* offers a countercultural way into and through the experience of grief, recognizing the vitality that can come when we welcome rather than reject the work and transformation that it can bring.

Through poetry and prayer, *Shelter in This Place: Meditations on 2020* offers a variety of reflections in a variety of voices on the experiences of loss, grief, and resilience.

Recovery and Resilience

If you are looking for something to help you keep going when the journey of recovery feels long and lonely, let me suggest these poems and resources to keep you company and cheer you on:

"A Litany for Survival" by Audre Lorde

"Power" by Adrienne Rich

"The Journey" by Mary Oliver, from her book *Dreamwork*

"Not without Longing," by Karen Benke, first published in *Sister*

"A Theology Adequate for the Night" by Nancy Shaffer and her collection *Instructions in Joy* offer poems that highlight daily brushes with the divine and the many ways that joy and grief intertwine in our lives.

Dr. Clarissa Pinkola Estés's "Do Not Lose Heart, We Were Made for These Times"

Ella and Penguin Stick Together by Megan Maynor is the book my daughter and I returned to at bedtime night after night that first year after our house fire. In this simple and sweet story, two friends show us how connection and a longing for wonder and joy can hold us through some of the hardest times.

If you are up for more in-depth learning, and whole books don't scare you off, here are a few of my trusted guides, guidebooks, and resources for understanding trauma, recovery, and resilience:

For an accessible summary that includes current and past research and a variety of stories that illustrate the many ways that trauma happens and the most current understandings of how to create healing opportunities for yourself and others, Dr. Bruce Perry and Oprah Winfrey's book, *What Happened to You?: Conversations on Trauma, Resilience, and Healing*, is a great place to start.

First published in 1992, Dr. Judith Herman's book *Trauma and Recovery: The Aftermath of Violence—from Domestic Abuse to Political Terror* shifted the story—and the clinical understanding and treatments that followed—for people who have experienced trauma of all kinds.

Dr. Bessel van der Kolk's 2014 book *The Body Keeps the Score: Brain, Mind, and Body in the Healing of Trauma* updates earlier understandings of trauma, resilience, and recovery and offers healing modalities outside of psychotherapy that survivors can use to support their healing. Singing, music making, dance, creative expression, yoga, ritual, and other actions that connect breath to body and help us know ourselves as one important part of a larger whole can all help.

In *My Grandmother's Hands: Racialized Trauma and the Pathway to Mending Our Hearts and Bodies*, Resmaa Menakem expands our understanding of trauma and recovery to include racialized and generational trauma, exploring the ways that injury and experience can continue to influence us and others and how we can heal.

In their book *Burnout: The Secret to Solving the Stress Cycle*, sisters Dr. Emily Nagoski and Amelia Nagoski explore contemporary experiences of stress and trauma and how to create and nurture the everyday habits and patterns that help to interrupt the stress cycle and foster health.

Memoirs are another way in, as we journey with the authors through their stories, often witnessing through them the power of writing, and rewriting, the stories that define us:

Somebody's Daughter: A Memoir by Ashley C. Ford takes us on a journey of self-understanding, acceptance, and joy as the author writes and rewrites her own stories of trauma, resilience, and the sometimes complicated relationships that can save us and help us know ourselves anew.

Nowhere Girl: A Memoir of a Fugitive Childhood by Cheryl Diamond takes us on an international tour of the world as the author experiences, uncovers, and understands her family and her life in new and fuller ways as she moves from childhood to adolescence to adulthood. Complex relationships and the grit of survival make up the substance of resilience and recovery in this unusual but still relatable story.

The Electric Woman: A Memoir in Death-Defying Acts by Tessa Fontaine takes us on an unusual journey of denial, understanding, and grief as the author joins the last touring sideshow in America and learns how to do everything from eating fire and charming snakes to living on the road in less-than-ideal conditions with strangers. In unexpected and disarming ways, the author's carnival life elicits lessons for the larger audience about love and what it takes to live a full life.

In *Waking: A Memoir of Trauma and Transcendence*, Matthew Sanford shares the story of a terrible car accident that changed his life forever and the journey that took him from near death to a whole and full life. His search for healing stories that helped him connect to his body and mind led him to new pathways for recovery.

Approaching the world—and ourselves—in an intentional and compassionate way can make all the difference when we are trying to foster resilience and recovery. These resources continue to shape me and my approach to myself and others.

The language we use to describe our experiences, ourselves, and each other matters. Approaching ourselves and everyone around us with compassion is a lifelong spiritual practice, and one great place to start is with the work of Dr. Kristen Neff (self-compassion.org).

In *A Hidden Wholeness: The Journey Toward an Undivided Life*, Quaker author Parker Palmer shares strategies for creating circles of trust, a specific kind of relational container where the deeper places in our soul can come out and thrive. While the techniques are specific to creating these particular kinds of communities, I've found that the advice in here—about creating gracious time and space, approaching important topics on the slant, welcoming art and creativity, and so much more—is all helpful in caring for myself and others.

Maybe a little humor helps you as much as it helps me. Buddhist teacher and author Jack Kornfield shares stories and strategies for wholehearted living in his classic text *After the Ecstasy, the Laundry: How the Heart Grows Wise on the Spiritual Path*.

And last but not least, maybe yoga will be a way of healing for you in your own way, just as it has been for me. If you are wondering where to start, you appreciate an intentionally antiracist, antioppressive, body-positive teacher and community, and swearing doesn't make you uncomfortable, let me suggest connecting with my home bases: Elisabeth Pletcher, a trauma-informed curvy yoga instructor (elisabethpletcher.com), and Yess Yoga, a trauma-informed Minneapolis-based studio and Registered Yoga Teacher yoga school (yessyogastudio.com).